WHITE EAGLE ON
THE INTUITION AND
INITIATION

White Eagle on the
INTUITION
AND INITIATION

WHITE EAGLE PUBLISHING TRUST
NEW LANDS · LISS · HAMPSHIRE · ENGLAND

First published 2004
Reprinted with corrections 2006

British Library Cataloguing-in-Publication Data
A catalogue record for this book is available from
the British Library

ISBN 978-085487-154-4

Printed in Great Britain by
Cambridge University Press

CONTENTS

INTRODUCTION

The intuition is an active, and sometimes surprising, force in most of our lives. If we find that an intuitive feeling about something—a flash of inspiration or unexpected realization—turns out to be correct, it can affect us quite deeply. Sometimes this intuition is accompanied by a prompt to action or change, either in ourselves or in how we manage our environment. However, as White Eagle says of such a feeling: 'It takes courage to act on it'. Yet when the action or change turns out to be just right—often in a remarkable way—the emotions within us leap in recognition of something greater and wiser than the ordinary, everyday self.

White Eagle says more than once in this book that to be told that we are soul and spirit foremost, even to be given proof of it through a medium or seer, is not the same thing as knowing it for ourselves. It is through the intuition (the inner spiritual wisdom) that we find the proof we need that we are more than mortal body and mind, and that there is a wise plan in operation for our lives. This plan may lead us in ways we do not understand.

The intuition is not something that only a few people can access. It is the link with our higher self, and thus open to all, but the conditions have to be right. Those conditions are not necessarily deep meditation and seclusion, but can be a state of being which we can set up and continually seek to maintain within ourselves throughout our daily life. Sometimes, because of this, the intuition can arrive in a flash, when we are in the middle of something quite mundane. We often ignore or quickly forget this intuitive flash in the press of everyday life. However, if we can learn to have a continual awareness of spirit, we can learn to remember and use our intuitive moments. This does not mean wandering around in a dream. It can be done in a most practical manner while getting on with our lives. With some effort we can also 'practise the presence of God' as we do so, so that this state of being becomes second nature.

In this book, White Eagle gives us help in doing just this. He gives insight into what the intuition is, so that we can more easily recognize it. He also shows us how it is related to our soul growth, and makes clear the distinction between intuition and our earthly mind, brain and emotions. Therefore, the book is divided into two main sections. The first concerns the nature of the intuition, while the second explores how we can develop this most useful faculty.

White Eagle has linked intuition with the unfoldment of the soul of humanity—the feminine energy within us all; and with the return to a greater understanding of the Divine Mother, which is part of the growth of humanity towards peace and brotherhood in the age of Aquarius. A short section at the end of the book therefore contains some of White Eagle's teaching about world peace, and how this can be achieved through the inward and outward healing work we can do. Through inner understanding—the gift of the intuition—we can work upon our own psyche and upon our relationships, both with others and with the earth herself. Because of this connection the reader will find the book entitled WHITE EAGLE ON DIVINE MOTHER, THE FEMININE, AND THE MYSTERIES, which appears as a companion to this one, to be well worth reading next.

The very word explains itself. In-tuition—training inside your self. You are looking outside for help, and all the time the help you want is inside. The world of spirit that so many of you talk about and believe in, and long to touch, is all within.

White Eagle, THE QUIET MIND

PART ONE:
WHAT THE INTUITION IS,
AND IS NOT

I

TRUTH

The Nature of Truth

BELOVED brethren, we meet to search for truth. We come from the realms of spirit, but have walked the earth path; and we try to give some of the knowledge which we have found. This is no easy task, because it is rarely possible for one soul to give truth to another. We cannot travel the path which is yours on your behalf, but we can act as a signpost, and tell you from our own experience where that path will lead. Yet the freewill choice is yours. Every soul is blessed with discrimination and discernment, and it is for the soul to use these faculties. One thing, however, is quite certain: truth, real truth, can only be discerned from the innermost, the pure spirit. This is why the Master so clearly advised His disciples and hearers to become as little children, which means to draw aside from that earthly or reasoning mind. Some will not agree with this. They say, 'But reason is given to us for a certain purpose'. Yes, your reason has its purpose, but it does not enable you to discern spiritual truth. Spiritual truth, when it is revealed by the Christ within, by the vision of the spirit, will pass all the tests of reason because it is unanswerable. When once the soul has discovered spiritual truth with the inner vision, there is no more questioning; because this truth satisfies everything in a person's being.

When we talk to you, we do not attempt to deal with knowledge already accumulated by the minds of men and women on earth. In order to catch a glimpse of universal truth, truth which will fit into every cranny of reason, you too must seek beyond the controversy of human statement and opinion. We know your difficulties; we fully recognize the limitations of mind; but we also see the inner self, which can rise above the bondage of the mind of earth. This inner self can, in a flash of intuition, arrive at truth, and do so without walking ponderously along a road which may end in a cul-de-sac.

We would explain to you all that we do not work on the purely mental or mind plane when we come, but on the intuitional or Buddhic plane of consciousness. The master Buddha was vibrating on the wisdom ray entirely: and his pupils, or *chelas*, found mastership through wisdom, through contemplation, through withdrawing from the world, and following the intuition, or the wisdom of the stillness within.

Likewise, when you wish to hear spiritual teaching, it is necessary for you to relax. Be still in mind, for when we bring through this knowledge from the higher planes, we need your inner attention too. We speak not from the plane of human knowledge, but from that of intuition, and we have to put into words truths almost incomprehensible to the earth mind. Our message is to be read not so much in the phrases used as in the spiritual power imparted. Proof of spiritual things is not possible, and only your intuition will uphold what we have to say.

Trust your own Truth

We claim no more authority for speaking as we shall, than you have in thinking according to your own intuition. We do not say ours is the only truth, but that according to our vision, this is what we see. Accept nothing that we say unless the light within guides you to do so. Indeed, *never* accept blindly what another soul says. Learn from your intuition.

Do not listen to what White Eagle says, and accept this as the only truth. I can teach you *nothing*, my brothers, my sisters. I may open your eyes; but you must through your own intuition find the path. Do not be persuaded by this or that person—they may be wrong. They invariably *are* wrong! You alone are right, because within you God speaks. The same is true for everyone.

Let us set this clear at once; it is not the *mental* part of you which is right. Indeed the lower mind, sensitive to the influence of others, will lead you astray. The higher mind, directed by the intuition or wisdom, will guide you to truth. When what you call truth comes through intuition and vision, it must indeed be true. Your brother's or sister's version of truth may be different, but it will be equally true. No-one can claim his or hers as the whole and only truth.

There are paradoxes which you continually meet on the spiritual path. Sometimes, we know it feels as though at every step there is a paradox. It is so confusing that you do not know what is meant, or which path you should take. Here again people are liable to lay down hard-and-fast rules. One says 'We must go that way!'. Another says 'No, this is the path—I *know*'. What are you to do? You are faced with a deep spiritual problem, and you have eventually to learn by your intuition to discriminate between what are sometimes described as the upper and the lower, or the left-hand and the right-hand paths. Here you cannot be bound by another's advice, because what is right for him or her, what is his or her pathway, is not necessarily yours. You must decide for yourselves which is the way to journey.

Yes … discrimination. *Everyone knows our duty but ourselves!* 'If I were you, I should do so and so!' Have you heard that? 'If I were Ms So and So, I should take this course.' *But would you?* If you were placed in exactly the vibrations, the conditions, and with the same qualities of soul-development, would you do as you say you would? How *can* anyone judge for another soul, whose quality of consciousness, whose feelings and reactions, are vastly different from their own?

You cannot decide for anyone else, and no-one else can decide for you. So, when these little arguments crop up, smile and say 'Yes … I know.' Say nothing to hurt the person who is so eager to advise you. Do not say, 'Oh no, I know that is not my path, you are quite wrong.' Say 'Yes.… ', but retain your inner knowing. And don't forget the smile!

Are we encouraging you to be deceptive? No. Men and women on earth need to wear masks at times. Yet they also need so to develop their 'x-ray vision' that they see through the mask to the real person beneath. When they can do this, they do not judge, they understand and have a feeling of goodwill and fellowship for everyone.

The Path to the Mysteries

It is rightly said that there is no new truth. We would add that all truth is contained within God. God is within you, but at present in you only as a seed, a seed-atom. But with the advance of humanity this seed will commence to grow, and you will find a dawning heavenly life, not in some far-off place but within your own temple, within your heart.

As we bring through to the earth plane our knowledge or revelation to help humanity, we find it very difficult to clothe inner truths in earthly language and pictures. We can convey a certain amount to you without words. We contact the halls of wisdom, and there is a line of communication down through the spheres, to an earth channel or instrument. But when our message comes right down into your midst, it has to come through an earthly vessel to an audience that is very limited—with apologies to you—but *of necessity* limited in its power to comprehend these inner secrets or mysteries of heaven. We in spirit are indeed handicapped by this.

Because we contact the halls of wisdom, the power of heaven comes with us; and those of you who are sensitive are able to catch a little of the light here and there. Your own vision opens; and although you yourself cannot put truth into words, you feel an inner knowing as you grasp these truths, these mysteries of God. This, of course, has always been the case, and as you read the Bible or any of the other great scriptures of the world, you will gradually uncover these age-old secrets. Yet until such secrets are uncovered, you will be left without an answer to many of your questions.

Today all people are free to follow the path, if they will, towards the mysteries. Some may speed and others loiter. Yet once you desire wisdom, not for your own satisfaction, not because of curiosity, but that you may labour to serve the whole earth, then your feet are placed on the path which leads ultimately to the house of light. And so, out of the great longing within your heart to serve, you find yourself. Once this happens, your soul is assisted with teaching, with guidance from the invisible. If you try and sample too many paths, you will find each one of them leads to a cul-de-sac; we say, therefore you are better to abide on the one path. Follow the one path, giving service: follow the light and guidance from your invisible teachers, and then the mysteries of the invisible worlds will be revealed to you. There are many ways of serving, and no student is bound to follow the path set by others; you should follow the light which shines from your own spirit.

Remember, then, the very first indication of truth, of true teaching, is simplicity. Simplicity first, and then profundity. Call to mind the simple and yet profound revelation of the Master Jesus; and that of the Lord Buddha. Look, then, for simplicity first in all revelation. Then follow it diligently; put into practice the actual *being* ... being and becoming in very truth those beautiful truths which have been revealed. Don't seek for short-cuts into the temple. There can be no gate-crashing ... only a steady upward climb, during which many a test must be passed.

The particular training which took place in the temple of the olden days, the seclusion and isolation which enabled the student finally to graduate, is gone. Today your life must be spent in a workaday world. People in what you call developed society are not shielded from the temptation of the outer world. Rather, the student is subject to the continual pull of the lower world, of excitements and the passions of the physical life. In former days, he or she withdrew, quietly pursued the path, worked diligently, and gave healing to the sick and comfort to those who mourned. Powers came which enabled him or her to draw aside the veil between their world and the invisible worlds. These same powers can be yours today. But you must literally go forth to the battlefield of life, and there learn to discriminate between the false and the true, between the real and the unreal. Oh, we know it! It is not easy!

Many of you on earth today were once workers in the Egyptian temples, particularly those of you who now serve in some simple and humble centre of spiritual light. Those drawn to such places have already learned certain inner truths which abide; because while the physical life passes, and even the personality brought onward from the past to a future life is dropped and hung up in the 'wardrobe' above (there to wait until required for use), the inner wisdom once learned from a mystery school is never lost. That is why many of you feel the stirring—the Ancient Wisdom—within your breast. You do not need to be convinced. Once you have seen into the invisible world, you *know*.

Meanwhile, we can only hint. We can only say things that will stir and quicken your minds and hearts so that you will catch a train of thought or intuition and follow that intuition. Spiritual truth is fluid. You can get principles upon which to work, but truth is like a great river with many tributaries. You will get sidetracked, you may get lost, but always you will come back to the main theme, the main principle. If you can rise above the earth and look down, you will see where all the

tributaries flow, see them all fit into the grand pano-
rama of beautiful life on earth, the Garden of Eden.

We too have only caught a glimpse of the grandeur
of the universe, only a brief insight into the possibilities
which lie within all. But such knowledge as we have
garnered in our meditations we give to you, as it may
prove a signpost on your own journey—along your path
of eternal progress and eternal unfoldment, leading to
eternal light and glory.

The spiritual universe may indeed be beyond your
comprehension, but from what we have seen of it,
we can only tell you it is glorious, overwhelming and
unbelievable to those who have yet to comprehend the
love of God. To describe it any further is like trying
to pour a great volume of liquid through a very small
funnel. You see, what we have to say does not bring
with it proof that the worldly mind accepts. The only
proof of these spiritual truths is that by the way of life
you live, you receive the proof and the demonstration
of truth. To put it in very simple language: the truths
work; and they work in the tiniest detail of your everyday life. You can all prove them for yourselves, but we
cannot prove them for you. Any living man or woman
can prove them if they like to apply the law to their
daily lives. As they do so, they can see the glory of the
heavens; they can realize the happiness of the spirit.

II

MOVING BEYOND THE AGE OF REASON

TIME IS nothing. Look back across two thousand years with true vision, and it is but yesterday; indeed, no more than a second flashing by. The age of reason has proved of great aid to human kind. You have heard it said by us that the reasoning mind must be laid aside; but we would not decry reason, because we know the importance, the value of mind, of intellect. When these tools have served their purpose, however, they should be allowed to grow into something greater, and that which has been of great value for centuries in bringing to humanity increasing individual conscious-ness, has now to be superseded by deeper intelligence and intuition.

You must pursue your path of contemplation; study and penetrate through intuition to the inner mysteries; but bear always in mind that the old beliefs contain for you a pearl of great price. See that you do not throw away the pearl—but rather, that you break open the casket to reveal the beauty of the jewel within.

The mission of the Master Jesus was to prepare human kind for the Aquarian Age. When they were given, at the start of the Piscean Age, his teachings were interpreted purely on the emotional, mental and material plane. It is the work of all of you who follow our teaching and who work on the ray of John[1] to unfold these mysteries. Once people open their hearts to the spirit, for instance, they will understand the spiritual meaning of the gospels.

The first essential towards this understanding is for the soul to surrender to God's love. It is a great temptation to insist upon reason being satisfied before such a surrender of the soul to the light of Christ within, or the voice of Christ, which is intuition. What you call cold reason can tempt the soul away from heavenly truth or divine intelligence. We almost dare to say that it is better to listen to intuition and be guided by pure innermost feeling, even if you do not fully understand where it is taking you, than to lose the way altogether by succumbing to the tempter, the mind. We do not of course mean the higher mind, because that is the instrument of the spirit.

In the Aquarian age, people will be stimulated both mentally and spiritually. There is a certain danger in mental stimulation, because the finite mind of a person demands exact truth, and yet truth is something that only the infinite mind can comprehend. It is impossible for any language on earth to satisfy the earthly mind on spiritual questions, because such questions can only be answered with the gradual evolution of the soul. The answers only come with the unfolding vision that develops in the course of spiritual progress for every soul. The demand that reason be satisfied will become ever stronger in the new age. Reason is growing, and it desires satisfaction; but along with it there comes in the new age a spiritual blessing which is intended to stimulate the intuition and to encourage the inner voice and the inner hearing of people. Until a person has acquired a certain degree of intuition and inner vision, the questions that he or she will be asking will be unanswerable. Reason can *only* be satisfied as intuition unfolds.

This is why there comes to the earth at the present time a pioneering ray of wisdom and love from afar. There are on earth at the present time those souls who can respond to this pioneering ray of spiritual knowledge and power, and they are destined to be the vanguards of the new religion.

As humanity becomes prepared for them, the mystery schools of the past will come again to the earth. We shall see upon the mountaintop the great white temple for prayer, meditation, and the creative power within people.[2] Thus the universal brotherhood of spirit will be established upon earth. There are those from the Piscean Age responding to the intuitional influence; those of whom the master spoke: *And your young men shall see visions* ... visions of what is to come, of the New Jerusalem. *And your old men shall dream dreams* ... meaning that they, too, in their dreams, would come under the beautiful influence of the rays of Neptune. Why are the planets Neptune and Uranus being drawn into the system of the earth's evolution over the present period? For this: for the sustenance of humanity; to usher in the age of the spirit, the age when the spirit of all people will function freely and *consciously* in higher worlds, while still in contact with the flesh.

You may be asking now if this means that you must lay aside reason and not be guided by it. We should prefer to say that when you have learned to hear the voice of spirit within, your reason will not take primary place. Reason will have served its purpose in your life, and its domination will pass away, like all other things do, when their purpose has been fulfilled. Out of *reason* will come *intuition*, or the divine intelligence of the God-self. But unless you give intuition an opportunity to grow and develop in your soul, you will respond for a long time to the harsh note of reason, and be bound in its chains.

People are so desirous of having everything cut and dried to satisfy the lower mind—the reason, the intellect—yet the inner truths lie beyond reason or intellect. Endeavour to train yourself to be receptive on the intuitional planes. One way of doing this is to keep what you are so fond of calling 'an open mind'.

Keeping an open mind will also preserve you in the Aquarian Age whenever there is a great uprising of the arrogant mind. Remember that every time this comes, there will be with it a great unfoldment of spiritual and soul power in humanity. When the body and soul of humanity is evolving, the mind is evolving—the higher mind—and the brain has to be prepared and developed so that the pure spirit can use the brain and help it comprehend the mysteries of the universe. Without that developed brain and higher mind, the spirit cannot get through to your consciousness—it cannot show you the beauty, truth, wisdom and love of those heavenly spheres of life. So you will see the mind getting very active and often very arrogant and powerful—becoming a driving force to get what it wants for itself and its body—for its physical life. But the next step will come and is coming, and that is the opening of the love in the heart. Recognition of love for creation, the unfoldment of love one for another, acting not for self alone: all this will come.

III

THE LOVE–WISDOM RAY

THE TIME has now come for men and women to develop a sixth sense, which we call intuition. For a long time now, people have concentrated upon the stimulation and development of intellect. This sixth sense, or ray of light, is destined to open for each one the secrets of nature, of creation, and all spiritual life and purpose. We ourselves work especially on this ray of intuition—the love–wisdom ray.[3] And so when you and we and the company of spiritual brethren meet together, we meet in love: desiring one of the most precious gifts of life, which is wisdom, through love.

We offer you a few thoughts. You may, by following the path of intuition, be led upward; but we ask you to remember that cosmic mysteries must remain inexplicable to the intellect. It is only when the light of the divine spirit of the pure love–wisdom ray enters that a person can glimpse these mysteries; and it is not yet possible for you to comprehend them entirely. This we ask: do not reject some of the thoughts which come to you like this, but rather store them for future consideration.

Many schools find the intellectual their path; it is

so because the intellect itself has a need to grow and expand. But there are those in incarnation who do not need to pass along the intellectual path in order to gain or absorb the eternal truths. Many find the way of the heart the easier. We work on the love–wisdom ray, and so we would reveal, not in words alone, but in essence, the glorious light of the spirit.

With the gaining of wisdom and understanding through love, humanity comes into the full power of its creation, which is Godhood. Let love–wisdom be your keynote, then, since it is by attuning yourselves to this vibration that you will absorb the inner wisdom of the mystery schools of all ages. Many approach the mysteries through intellectual striving and so gain much knowledge; they read facts and interpret symbols, but no-one can go on for ever without meeting that shining mystery which has to be read not in the mind, but with wisdom.

Many people secretly regret their lack of mental training and intellectual attainment (or what the world calls 'education'); yet these same people may have within them the right aspiration ... intuition. To them we say: 'Regret nothing; if the powers that be, the great Lords of Karma, had seen fit to place you in conditions of life which would have brought intellectual attainments and a comprehensive education, you would have been so placed'. There are many on earth at present who in past lives have stored within them all that education and intellect could bestow. During this incarnation, therefore, their development lies along the love–wisdom, or intuitional, path. This leaves the physical brain unclouded, and thus the wisdom stored within the soul can register in the outer consciousness, or be reflected there. We repeat: regret nothing. Accept the conditions of life as they present themselves with a thankful heart, knowing them as necessary for you at the present time.

There are, after all, many ways of learning the inner mysteries, and not all of them involve written or spoken words. If the soul can attune itself to higher planes of love and wisdom, the mind in the heart will absorb what is there. Then, although the outer mind does not always interpret the truth thus absorbed immediately, nevertheless later the mind *will* begin to interpret and in time know great truths. The heart does not register incorrectly. *That which the heart absorbs is truth.* In this present age, this sense called intuition is developing; through the intuition, hitherto insoluble truths will be solved—truths insoluble to the materialist, however great his or her intellect. The mind of the heart will *know*, will understand, these greater mysteries.

Buddha was on the Wisdom ray, Jesus was on the Love ray. Wisdom, love and power—the three aspects of the Deity. There were those earlier who manifested on the ray of power. Power, wisdom and finally love; and through love humanity is redeemed.

IV

REALIZING THE SOURCE: THE CHRIST WITHIN

THE SOUL'S awakening, its initiation, is related not only to the Christian teaching but also to other religions all down the ages. The soul's awakening is the Ancient Wisdom. It is a jewel which has many facets: many, many aspects. We would emphasize again that all this knowledge is not only interesting but fascinating to the mind. Therein lies the danger. It is no use becoming engrossed intellectually; what you need is a full realization of the light within yourself; and you need actually to become that light. Again and again, we find we need to emphasize to you the importance of starting all investigation and research on the spiritual planes from the one humble and simple truth—which is the Christ within yourself.

There is no religion higher than truth, as you are told; and truth comes from the Son of God, and the Son of God is Christ.[4] Christ is pouring His rays upon all people. They flow from the Heart of the Son of God, from Christ the Lord, to the heart of everyone, but the majority close themselves and cut themselves off from those living rays. When the individual cuts away that line of inspiration and intuition, and clothes itself round with the lower wrappers of the desire body and of the physical and lower mental bodies, truth struggles in vain for life and activity.

Many of you have heard about the Aquarian Age, upon which humanity is now embarking, and about the Seventh Ray, whose influence will be particularly felt during this Aquarian Age. This Seventh Ray is recognized to be the ray of the higher psychic development, of ritual, of ceremonial, of brotherhood. In other words, this is the age for the development of inner or soul powers. But the Seventh Ray work takes other forms. It is connected also with the development of physical science.

God is omnipotent. The Seventh Ray is guarded, protected by the Wise Ones who act under Divine Wisdom and Power. But at the same time, in order to assist the true unfoldment of human spiritual power and the right application of science, both psychic, spiritual and material, it is necessary that human knowledge should be balanced by the indwelling spirit of the Christ.

Therefore, when we repeat, many times, that the teachings which come from the Christ are indeed the universal teachings of love, we do so because it is vitally necessary for all peoples to grow strong in love, and to be balanced through knowledge of the spiritual law which is working throughout all life. Humanity's enemy is arrogance. People think they know what they want and what is good for them. You have yet to learn the lesson which the Master Jesus not only taught but demonstrated, that of meekness and humility. Many, many times you have heard us say that first you must love God. Your conscious unity with the Divine Spirit is the foundation of everything.

While the Age of Aquarius is a mental age, it is also a spiritual age. For this reason, you tread a difficult path as you enter it, one which is like a razor's edge. You will come up against many difficult situations not only in your individual life, but also in your national life. We of the Brotherhood in the world above return to you for one purpose, which is in order to help you to awaken to the knowledge of spiritual life, and of the initiations which you undergo on the spiritual path.

People often ask what is meant by initiation. Initiation is an awakening of the spirit in people; and not only the awakening but a continuation of the unfoldment and development of the Christ power within an individual. It means an expansion of consciousness to reveal the heavenly mysteries. Before this esoteric knowledge can be imparted and humanity is able to use those occult powers rightly, you must each be tested and tried in your faith and trust in God's love and wisdom.

The answer to the problems of every soul is to surrender to the Will of God. 'Thy Will be done, O God!'. But this surrender is very difficult for those of you who are setting out upon the spiritual path, particularly when you think you know more than you can

truly understand. Then you get confused with material problems in your life. This is precisely where you are being tested. The present time is bringing you enhanced faculties and greater opportunities to discriminate between what is true and what is false. Only through such diligent and humble searching for Christ within will you find what you seek.

If you pursue the path of truth, if you live earnestly and ask for revelation, it will come. God never fails. What you will need is discernment, so that you can truly recognize truth. Only the God or the Christ in your heart will enable you to recognize Christ in the world outside, or behold Christ in another being. By their fruits ye shall know the great ones; their keynote is humility and simplicity; they make no great claims of any kind. You will know them by the light in the eyes, gentleness in the speech, truth in the action—by the unmistakeable sign of the true and the beautiful. And when you make contact with them on the higher mental plane, you will do so *by virtue of the spirit or the Christ within your own heart,* which is pure and holy, and wholly true. This is the centre from which all aspirants must work.

Do not be misled into thinking that you can remain for ever complacent, thinking that all things will work out eventually for your comfort and peace and happiness. Really to tread the path you need to be prepared to find it at times a knife-edge. You must work both inwardly and outwardly; you need in one way or another to pray for guidance; and you must also daily partake of the inner communion, the inner breaking of bread. You know this, but the demands of modern life claim you and distract you from the need to live consciously, always inwardly present. Observing this need while at the same time giving loving service in the world will build into your being particles of light, transmuting the darkness, and overcoming the destructive forces that play around and within you. This is the secret the illumined ones have: the wisdom that has always been waiting for humanity to find. It is the secret of the transmutation of the dark, dull, heavy metals of gross matter into the pure gold of spiritual substance. Yes, the spirit world, the celestial world, the higher astral world, is built of spiritual substance that is composed entirely of the rays of light of the spiritual Sun. This is why the Lord Christ is the saviour of the world: because it is the spirit of Christ, the giver of all love and wisdom, which stimulates in the human heart aspiration for the light of heaven.

Remember that development of the mental body depends upon your habitual thought. We mean by this the building or development of the higher mental vehicle through which the Christ within can and will operate, so as to create a world so far removed from and above this earth that it will not be of the same substance. Think of yourselves as descending like a babe to this earth in order not only to develop in yourselves the qualities of the Son of God, but in the process to

help all people to develop, and to look towards the Great Light for their happiness and their redemption. Redemption, we would say, means their return or escape from the darkness of lower matter to the freedom of the sun-world, the Christ kingdom.

Through meditation, prayer and aspiration, you can rise in *thought,* in your higher mental body, above this physical plane. You can function *consciously* in the heaven world. You need not die before you pass through the Second Death—the leaving-aside altogether of the earth personality. You can enter the heaven world in full consciousness, even though living in the body of flesh.

Until this time, your eyes are sealed, and your ears are stopped, and you do not know; for you walk in a state of darkness. Therefore in the mystery school of life, the first question the candidate is asked is this: 'What is your dearest wish, your greatest need, my brother or my sister?' And the one entering upon the path answers: *'Light!* … the key of creation … the magical light!'. Train yourselves, then, to seek to be power stations to receive and transmit the light of the Christ within.

In the heaven world, there is no separation; and while all people retain their individuality, they are as drops in the ocean. All of life moves forward as one grand universal brotherhood. This is one of the secrets of the white magic: brotherhood. The simplest teaching, and yet the gravest and most profound, came from the master Jesus, when He said: *Love one another.... Love the Lord thy God with all thy heart and soul and mind, and thy neighbour as thyself.*[5] It is impossible to live in splendid isolation: either with or against your will, you are affecting the lives of millions by your attitude of thought.

V

THE NATURE OF THE INTUITION

Spiritual Consciousness

IN YOUR Bible, it says that God created man in His own image, and it has become the habit to regard God as being like a human being. But what is the inner meaning? God created man and woman alike in the divine image—each of them a spirit with spiritual qualities, a spiritual likeness to God. If you are God's child, the son–daughter of God, as you are clearly told, both in the Old Testament and in the New, you will see that a man or woman is a being with Godlike potentialities.

God is to a human the highest being that he or she can conceive. So it has become your habit to think of God as a genial and pleasant kind of super-person, because until your spiritual consciousness has developed, your powers are limited. Nevertheless every one of you, being a child of God, has all the Godlike potentialities within. You have come from God as a spark of the divine fire; within that spark lies the potential to kindle a divine fire as great as that from which it came. A spark from one fire resting on suitable material can cause a big blaze. Therefore, having come from God, being part of God, you know that by your attunement to the Godlike you have the potential to become a glorious being. That spark of the divine fire has travelled down through the spheres of light—down, down, down into the very depths of matter. All the time it has been descending it has been learning, gaining in consciousness of its own power.

All which is breathed forth by God passes through every one of the realms of life in its growth and evolution. Life rises through all the realms to the human and divine; only there are different paths, different journeys which certain groups of souls make. We could not trace all these journeys for you, but groups take their separate paths according to their nature and purpose. By one path or another, you must traverse all these realms, and will eventually know them all: the worlds below as well as the worlds above.

When you begin to open the spiritual consciousness, you will find that all the worlds are now open to you consciously, whereas before you have passed through in the unconscious state. When you receive illumination with the Divine, you re-traverse all these stages at will. You can go through the mineral, the animal, and the vegetable levels of life. The inner planes are open to you to experience them consciously. You enter into them, you become part of them. Christ is in everything, God is in everything.

The God life is expressed in every form of matter on

your earth. You like to pick it out and segregate it and make everything compact. Think instead of life as one great unity. God is in everything, *you* are in everything; but you do not know it yet. The consciousness has to expand until the spirit within becomes conscious, not only of God but of all God's life.

Let us bring to mind also that the path of eternal progress is there for the soul *if the soul wills*. At first, it follows almost an instinctive urge towards growth. Then it comes to the point where there is a realization of its power of choice. At this point, by its actions, by its response either to what is called constructive or to the destructive—to good or evil—it makes its choice.

We shall deal as far as we can with the spiritual as well as the material advance that you can expect in the new age. First will come this consciousness of humanity's spiritual or soul powers. For several ages past, humanity has been going through a rather dark cycle, which has immersed people deeply in physical matter. People are now just rising from this state of darkness and beginning to see a glimmer of light. In the future this spiritual consciousness or God-consciousness will grow. Possession of these soul powers will be realized by the majority of people. An individual is both divine and human. Neither aspect must be neglected. It is of the utmost importance that the human side of the nature should be utilised in the right and true way as well as the divine nature, which also must be encouraged to grow in stature.

Necessary Limitations

The purpose of physical life is that each of us may bring the greater consciousness of the inner life, or the God life, through into manifestation through the physical. The limitations of the physical are the test that is necessary for this to take place. Through them, your power—we could call it your effectiveness—in bringing through the inner life to the outer, is gauged. You may experience the initiation in a higher state of consciousness. Illumination may indeed come then, but it will happen while life is still in the physical body. The physical body is as much part of God as the spirit—'as above, so below'. There cannot be separation, and that is the whole point of the path of initiation—the complete interpenetration of all these planes. God is as much in your physical body as in your higher spiritual consciousness, and though you may experience your illumination out of the body, you must be able to express it and live it—in the body.

You may wonder if it is possible for a soul to become spiritually developed in one incarnation, but then come back to earth with the developed part hidden or closed off? Certainly, it may be necessary for a soul to come back in a certain incarnation with other qualities of character more prominent than the ones already developed, because he or she may have service to give: for instance, on a more material plane. If his or her service to humanity lies perhaps in the world of business, it will be necessary for commercial instincts and gifts to have full play. The light from heaven would rather dazzle and divert the person from their course. So the light is mercifully veiled for the time being. We think this will indicate how impossible it is for anyone to judge another soul.

When the soul from whom the light has been temporarily obscured has accomplished the work they were doing, and learnt the lessons attached to it, it is quite likely that the spiritual light will flood his or her higher consciousness to such a degree that the ordinary consciousness becomes aware of it.

Which Path?

Some religions tend, through ritual, to stir the emotional aspect of the soul; and through the emotions to reach the spirit. Through emotion—or, better still, through intuition—one does reach the spirit.

As you consider your path, bear in mind that the soul is threefold in structure. We speak of the first aspect as the soul-consciousness, the personality; the second aspect as intellect, or thought, the part that functions on the mental plane; and the third aspect we speak of as the emotional or the intuitional.

Each one of these aspects or rays of the soul interpenetrate the three lower aspects of a man or woman, which are the physical aspects, just as they also reach to and penetrate the three higher aspects, which are those of the spirit. Through the physical aspect of a woman or a man the soul is fed; so also at the spiritual or spirit level the body aspect is inspired and urged forward to create material for the building of the soul. It is through the growth of feeling that the individual develops a soul.

As you learn to understand this ensouling process, you may see Christ becoming manifest in perfectly-evolved beings whom the world now hails as avatars. These may be ones you think of as the saviours of humanity, for they are born into the flesh to teach and to help the rest of humanity to develop those qualities that will enable each soul eventually to become impregnated by the divine spirit and itself bring forth the Christ-child.

Among the paths of soul-development which may lie in front of you are those you might distinguish as the occult, mystic and psychic paths. Which path are you to follow? How are you to judge? First, if you mean the path of the true psychic, we would couple that with the mystical. The true mystic must of necessity be psychic, because true psychic power is developed on that mystical path. So let us reduce these paths to the mystical and the occult only.

The mystical path is the path taken by the devotee, one who worships and loves an ideal, and has no thought of anything but his or her ideal, to which he or she adheres with a great love. Such a person contemplates and meditates on the light. He or she is the true mystic, following at all times the ideal of love, devotion and worship.

The occult path we would describe as bringing through, into the sphere of action, knowledge of the inner planes and the power lying behind physical manifestation. The occult path is the path of power, using the knowledge gained either for selfish or for selfless purposes. Therefore the occult path must be dangerous, because temptation is great. Ritual of the purest kind will raise the consciousness of the individual to a high plane of spiritual intuition. That is to say, it first raises the consciousness, then opens the intuition centre to the inflow of spiritual forces. If you normally gravitate towards the intuitional, if you feel intuition guides you, then you follow the mystical and the love–wisdom ray.

If your mind is uppermost, if you want knowledge and reason, and to know how to use the powers you have, then the occult path will attract you most. But eventually there must of course be harmony between the mind and the heart. The mystical path is the path of the heart, and the occult that of the head. The more you advance on either, you come at length to the same place. No, it makes no difference which path you take, so far as the final result is concerned, because in the end, all paths blend. On the mystical path you eventually learn all that which you would have learnt on the occult.

The True Self and the Outer Life

The Brotherhood in spirit would have you know that you must learn to distinguish between your inner self and your outer physical life, because the inability to separate the one from the other is in itself responsible for much of the confusion which confronts you. You must develop your spiritual being surely, strongly and purposefully, every day of your life: first by the practice of meditation, and secondly through the continual practice of love in your daily life.

Attached to the body-self (that is, the physical body, but with it the habitual thoughts, feelings, and instincts) is a certain form which is recognizable as the body-elemental. This is not an evil thing; it has its place in the evolution, not only of people, but in the evolution of the lower forms of life also. This body-elemental is very strong in most people, and you have to learn in the course of your evolution that the higher self (which is only partially in evidence in most of us) must gain complete domination over the body-elemental. The home of the 'I' is in the celestial body, the highest and purest being of a person; and the bidding of the 'I' descends to the consciousness as the intuition—something you may at times call conscience. The body-elemental is also assisting you in your evolution. We will for the moment call it the ballast which keeps you rather glued to the earth. You all feel this pull, but we would make clear to you that this is not to be regarded as evil; for by the reciprocal forces caused, you gradually rise above the lower self. The very pull of the body-elemental forces the growth of the spiritual or the God-consciousness which we come back to the earth to evolve.

The lower etheric body is interpenetrated by a finer etheric, which I will call the body of light, or the vital body. This vital body also interpenetrates the higher vehicles, the mental body, the intuitional body, and the celestial body. So we get a connecting link, a thread of light descending from the Christ sphere or plane of divine life, down through the various bodies into the dense etheric, the latter being the bridge which connects all the chain to the physical sense or brain of an individual.

We find connection between the etheric body and certain centres in the physical body. This connection is not only to the chakras but to the main lifestream in the physical body, which flows through the brain and spinal cord. The centres are in turn connected with the different spheres or planes of spiritual life.

The vital body is not really separate, but an emanation of the physical one. It departs with the death of the physical body, except for a small part which is drawn up into the highest aura—which we will call the celestial aura. Through its contact with earth this aura has absorbed certain lessons. These lessons are retained to be used in the future states of life, not necessarily in the heaven world, but in future periods of incarnation.

After the etheric, the next body to be seen is the

astral body. The astral, the mental and the celestial body between them comprise the soul. But there is something else; there is the spirit. We are coming into still higher realms. Try to follow what we will say to you about this pure spirit. You are familiar with what we tell you about the Holy and Blessed Three, the Holy Trinity, the Father–Mother–Christ, the Father–Mother and the Son, Christ. Now, when the soul has perfected itself—that is, has garnered all the experience it can from the physical life so that it is ready to pass on into the Christ initiation, there is a wonderful 'resurrection' awaiting it. The Christ in a man or woman becomes conscious, stirs, awakens. It was Christ himself who paved the way for humanity; he took this first wonderful Christ initiation, and Jesus was the great initiate for the manifestation of this Christ spirit. Jesus *became* the Christed one. He trod the path and demonstrated to humanity the way. He said: 'I *am* that way, that truth and life'. Jesus demonstrated to the rest of humanity *the way to life eternal*. Jesus Christ was not the only Christed one, but he did demonstrate the way of purification of the vehicles, of all the vehicles, including the physical, for every soul. Some people think that humanity depends upon the saving grace of Jesus Christ, and without Jesus Christ crucified on the cross humanity cannot save itself! This is not so. It is not the outer Christ that humanity is seeking, except as an example and demonstration. A man or woman has to find the inner Christ, and this comes with his or her second

birth. Some people would say the second death; because where there is death there must be birth; death
from this life means birth into the spirit life.

The Sixth Sense

As we move towards describing the sixth sense, let us
first consider what we will call the eight principles of
life. They are Earth, Air, Fire, Water, Ether, Mind or
Intelligence (which is the controlling power), the Soul
(or individualization), and Intuition or Spirit. Now
out of these principles five have correspondence or
relationship to a physical sense. Again through these
physical senses, a man or woman opens the way to the
inner mysteries of his or her being.

At one level, intuition is a sixth sense. At another, it
is the 'I' or the divinity within which knows everything
If the divinity within is sufficiently developed, it is all-
conscious and knows all things. When you reach the
intuitional or Buddhic plane, you see not with the brow
only, but with other centres. The heart centre commences to radiate, and you become 'aware' of truth.
When you get to this plane, you register or reflect the
spiritual worlds truly. At this stage, the whole body (not
the physical only, but the higher bodies too) is register-
ing, and you can see from any part. Indeed, the whole
being sees. In this respect, the sixth sense dispenses
with all the other senses.

This sixth sense is continually being developed, and

in the future it will become as natural to use as the other five. Meanwhile, the quickening or awakening of the sixth sense is a great step forward. Various names might be used, but we think that 'intuition' is the best word to describe this awakening to cosmic truth. We sometimes refer to it also as the inner light, which seems to guide you to certain action and onto certain lines of thought.

With development of intuition, it is the heart centre and the brow chakra, and lastly the crown of the head, which are being brought into operation. The intuition is only unfailing when it is selfless and when the human spirit is concentrating upon the Great Spirit. And this leads us to focus upon your everyday life and your human relationships, because it is your life, your relationships, your behaviour to each other, and your behaviour in your own temple, which is going to qualify you to work with your intuition. It is going to qualify you not only in the ability to see but also in the interpretation of what you see. You may be taken up into higher worlds, see many beautiful things; but if you do not have spiritual understanding, they remain just images and figures and no more.

Let us now consider these higher mental states of psychic unfoldment—in which, as we have told you, the three higher centres or chakras are used. In your meditation, you are being taught how to bring these higher chakras to life: how to open your consciousness to the pure level of life, which is superior altogether to the physical plane. In development of the chakras and the higher mind, the candidate learns how to make contact in the correct way, without danger. There is a right way to unfold the inner faculties, the sixth sense, which functions from the heart centre. In meditation, in true contemplation of the Deity and all that is holy (which means healthy and pure), you are opening up that heart centre. The safe way and the correct way for spiritual unfoldment is to work from the heart of love. In meditation, you are also opening the throat centre for pure speech and knowledge. This comes from the fifth sphere, the sphere of Mercury. With development of the throat centre comes inspiration for speech. Those who would themselves be teachers should quicken this, and receive through head and throat the divine inflow of wisdom and knowledge which they will give forth.

So you see the importance of the daily meditation: the preparation for the day which sets you up in thinking before you speak and act, the importance of the control of the temper and emotions? This, my brethren, is the way by which you unfold the powers of clear vision and clear hearing. You must cling, with all the power of God, to love and all the qualities of the Christ spirit. Then you will not be deceived; then you will not be inaccurate in what you see and hear. The sixth sense is the first sense which connects your spirit with the physical plane. This is what you are striving after in your development, which must start with meditation.[6]

More than one Mind

The masters teach us that if we would tread the path of the mysteries, we must train ourselves to think accurately, to take care of our surroundings, to create harmony, to be precise and particular in our thought. This is the foundation upon which a person's spiritual life is built. *The power of magic is the power which the individual can wield in thought.* In a small degree you are learning to use the white magic. However, the development of so-called psychic gifts may be only preliminary to the opening of spiritual gifts, or the power of the Christ innate in each soul. This power will in time hold dominion, and draw all people together in one grand universal brother–sisterhood. When this great assembly peoples the earth, the very vibrations, and the very physical conditions of the earth, will change. They will become finer and more etherealized. You have the power to contribute to this; to work henceforth for the furtherance of earth's humanity.

Most men and women live as in a little prison. They immerse themselves in the task of earning their daily bread—their food and clothing and their housing—and in protecting the body. Ignorance and fear keep them imprisoned. But ever more opportunities are to be given to human beings to awaken them from their deep sleep in materialism. There is a great pressure, or outpouring upon humanity in this age, the new age, which comes through the mental vibrations, through the power of thought stimulating the higher centres of your consciousness, the higher mind. The angelic hosts draw very close to humanity, pouring upon human beings rays of truth and light. You will notice from now on, and in every direction, revival and stimulation of the spiritual faculties in people. No longer will materialism hold sway. Evidence of spiritual forces will be seen in literature, music and science.

Remember that your mind is more than a simple instrument within the brain; the mind which normally functions on the material plane of life is a very small part of it. You may go through experiences on higher planes, but only be conscious within your spirit of a quickening of consciousness, a new sensitivity or awareness of spiritual forces. You may know only in your heart and in your inner self. If that spiritual self which is in direct contact with the universal spiritual power becomes illumined or quickened, the awareness is transferred to the feeling, the intuition of the individual, but not always to the brain.

We would guide and help you to be very strong and to allow your intuition (or the higher mind, which is another word you might use for intuition) at all times to be master of the earthly mind. The higher mind will never mislead. If you will be true to the higher mind in any problem which confronts your human life, you will get a correct and wise answer to guide you in making your decision.

Let us speak for a moment about the air initiation.

It is said that Mercury is the messenger of the gods. It is also said that Mercury is the ruler of the fifth world: that is, the sphere of the higher mind. Mercury is the messenger coming from higher spheres to bring truth to humanity. Mercury is also the ruler of Gemini, and the symbol of Gemini, as you know, is the heavenly twins, the two pillars. The soul has to pass through these two pillars into the temple of initiation. Shall we call these two pillars the mind and the intuition?—the higher mind, which is situated at the back of the head, and the frontal mind, the intellect or the mind of earth. In the air initiation, the neophyte has to see very truly and to pass between the pillars of the higher and the lower mind so that there is absolute balance, before it achieves the air initiation.

You all experience the conflict between these two minds, these two selves. Probably your greatest difficulty is the arguments of the worldly mind, for the arguments often sound so sane and right. There is always this pull. Do you remember the Master stilling the waves and commanding the winds to be still during the storm on the Sea of Galilee?[7] He commanded the turbulent winds of the lower mind, because the air represents the mind in its entirety (not the single aspect only; both aspects are symbolized by air). It is of vital importance for that mind of earth to be in abeyance and controlled by the mind of the intuition, the higher mind, the mind of Christ, the mind of the spirit.

Mistakes?

As your intuition develops, you may feel you may make mistakes in discriminating between the higher mind and the lower or outer mind. We all make mistakes in comparison with the greater and wiser ones above. In terms of your development, though, mistakes do not matter. Certainly it is right to strive to develop the intuition. Simply make sure that the inner voice comes from the heart of wisdom and not from the self that wants something, the desire self.

Often, intuition comes like a flash; it is an inward knowing. The thing is to have courage to act on it, to be prepared for whatever it brings. Then the intuition can be further developed in meditation: not through activity of the mind but through quiet contemplation within the sanctuary of the heart.

Some have asked the question, whether it is possible for anyone to make a major mistake—to take the wrong turning, to choose completely the wrong path. That is a wide question, which needs careful answering. We do not think that in an event affecting the whole incarnation, the soul can make a mistake. A deep intuition will urge the soul to take a certain path, and even if it appears to be wrong to all onlookers, the soul unconsciously knows that it has to tread that path, for karma is directing the soul. I think this would rank as one of the major pillars in the construction of the temple, and the soul could not go wrong. It is in little things that more play is given.

A soul may of course *think* it has taken the wrong path, because the choice leads him or her into a great deal of trouble. We think you will find that it is only the outer mind that might think like this, while the higher mind would know better. We are not so much concerned with the outer mind, as with the progress of the soul. The outer mind may decide that even with spirit guidance there has been a mistake made, but the outer mind does not understand all the spiritual laws lying behind the life of a person; it pulls in a different direction. In the case of any important event, there is a strong intuition at work, but the outer mind will argue and say 'my commonsense tells me it is wrong, not wise'. And yet something urges the soul onward. Sometimes, you know so well, trifling events—a careless word, the missing of a train, the picking up of a book—will change a whole life. You will say 'If it had not been for this trivial thing, the whole course of my life would have been different!' But the trivial thing has happened! The angels and the Lords of Karma have been watching closely. God has given *His angels charge over thee; ... they shall bear thee up, lest at any time thou dash thy foot against a stone.*[8]

VI

THE PURPOSE OF THE INTUITION

A Creative Atmosphere

WHEN YOU come into a place where spiritual truth is taught, many of you are impressed, not so much by what is said from the rostrum, as by the response you discover in yourself to something invisible. You may call it atmosphere, but you can feel it in your souls. Now feeling of this sort is the most important sense of all. It is usually overlooked, because men and women do not recognize in it the beginning of development of a sixth sense. When you feel an atmosphere, or feel love or kindness around you, you are touching or responding to the influence of an invisible world. This subtle sense of intuitive feeling is becoming developed in the new age of Aquarius, and with it grows brotherhood.

Christianity is a religion in which the emotions are stirred. They are made use of, for the emotional body is one vehicle through which the higher influences of heaven can reach a person. But in the Aquarian Age, it will be the higher spiritual body, the intuitional body, that will be used; and through the intuition a new creative spirit will come to humanity. You are preparing today. People who participate in any group centred on the new Age are being attuned, and so is the place in which you meet. You are sounding a tuning note, so that the forces of the higher worlds can be directed to that spot, to that group of people. Through these groups a note is sounded forth, not only on the earth, but on the astral plane. It is one which not only affects the people on earth, but also those who are awaiting incarnation, who are descending through the astral plane on their way back to rebirth.

Past Lives

In the heart mind lies the seed of all that has passed, and all that you are accumulating today in your physical, astral, mental, and celestial bodies—indeed, every one of the seven bodies of your being[9]—all that will be stored away in your heart-mind, where lies the memory of the past. All that you do today, which has left so deep and lasting an effect upon your soul, will be living in you tomorrow, in your next life.

From the mind in the heart comes cosmic wisdom and memory of the far past. These memories are also linked with the planetary influences, but planetary influences directed upon the present incarnation have their roots in the past, and are linked up with that wonderful mind of the heart.

On occasion, as you sit by your fireside, you may gaze

into the fire and, concentrating on it, read symbols in the flames. If you interpret such symbols—not with your mind, but through intuition and your spirit—you can prophesy the future. We use that as an illustration to show that the future, the past, rests in the here and now, and may be read by those who have vision.

Certainly, the memory of previous incarnations can be recalled, as the soul strives to reach the higher consciousness, outside the limitations of the physical brain. With many people, it is just a nebulous feeling. Or it may be that the soul is aware of certain tastes and characteristics brought back from the past—love of embroidery from China, love of dancing from Greece or Spain, love of Egyptian art. Some little trait in the character may betray a link with some past civiliza-tion. These memories do not come through the earthly brain, so much as through the spiritual brain, centred in the heart. It is through the mind in the heart that contact with eternity is made.[10]

You ask, 'Why cannot we remember our past lives?' What proof can you give us of the theory of reincarna-tion?' Spiritual things can only be proven in a spiritual way; no-one can give you proof of reincarnation or of spiritual truth. Proof of reincarnation can only come to you through your own intuition, from your own ex-perience. 'Why can we not remember the past?', you say. Wait; can you recall the time when you were aged two, three, four? I have heard a clairvoyant give descrip-tions which require you to go back ten or fifteen years perhaps, and you cannot remember even then all that happened. Much of it is a blank; your brain refuses to register. How then can you hope to remember, through the organism of the physical brain, incarnations of hundreds and thousands of years ago? Memory simply is not *in* this physical brain, not in the astral nor the mental bodies with which you have clothed yourself. When, however, you can function in the higher body (which some call the 'causal' body and which I will call the 'temple')—when you function thus, your vision will be opened and you will remember, because you will touch the mind which is the storehouse of all the past.

The Seeker

Egypt presents to our minds here a land of sunshine and light; not only the light of the physical sun, but the light of the spirit; because in prehistoric Egypt, truly the spirit was the interpreter, not the mind ... the spirit and the intuition were the interpreters of the greater mysteries of life. In this day of life, your intuition is awakening and urging you to seek, *seek* the light. So great is this desire that you go hither and thither in your search. Often, complete confusion is the result, for you encounter so many contradictions in your search. The mind is greedy. How you delight to hear any crumbs we can give you about life in Egypt! You delight to hear about your own incarnations, long to have greater knowledge of your own life in this past. This is all symptomatic.

When you are truly ready, through experience, to look into the mirror of your own soul, you will see just how agreeable—or the reverse—has been your past; and it takes a strong and wise soul to be able to face the truth. The difficult part is for a soul to live, day by day, in a dark world, absorbing the lessons which the outer life is intended to teach. There are no short cuts to the promised land. You may get a ladder (which is how we will describe the intellect for a moment) and run up it and peep over into the promised land, and see it flowing with milk and honey. There are many people who do just this. They look over and think they know; they think they have reached the promised land. But it is only an illusion. There is but one way to arrive at the promised land, and that is by becoming suitably clothed in raiment which is of the very substance of the promised land. This means that the soul can only know the promised land by becoming an inhabitant of it, by living patiently and happily and never losing sight of the guiding light from above, never allowing the light to go out in the heart. Thus the very simplest soul—a child indeed—can enter there.

If you would follow our guidance, you would not try to set about finding your past incarnations, because when you do so you may get a shock. Until you are ready to stand the shock, we suggest with some seriousness that you keep the door closed. There are many who think they know their past. It is true that the power of spirit is quickening in humanity, and many are having their consciousness or memory quickened. You cannot find anything about past lives through the lower mental vehicle, which you must already be using if you *want* to find out! When you can touch the Buddhic or the plane of pure spirit, it is there that you will find the memory and the storehouse.

At times during the night you may be taken to the Hall of Records, and in the moments immediately after waking you may bring back a flash, as in a dream. Take notice of your awakening moments. But you have to be quick, for after you wake it is forgotten in a flash. And it is good to fall asleep meditating upon the Divine Light, for then you may go to where you will be permitted to glimpse the past.

It is this becoming aware, or *being* light that will restore understanding and bring back memories of past lives. But these will not come through the head centre. Such memories well up through the mind of the heart. Within the heart centre lies the growing pearl, with the deposits of past incarnations. That pearl contains memories of past lives—past failures, past triumphs, even past characteristics which have become part of the soul. For the soul is like a hallowed building and its memories are eternal.

A Feeling for the Main Ray on which you Work

How can you know which is your particular ray? Back again we come to the same old guiding star—the intuition. Get beneath the layers of the outer self, and feel the inner self that will truly express the response from one of the seven rays. Listen for it. If you study your actions and ideals, these may confirm what your intuition says. What do you feel you want to do? Do you wish to heal, do you want to give in love, to share? Are you filled with a sense of brotherhood for all life? That is the Ray of Altruism. Is your instinct to meditate and pray, to turn to God—do you feel this? Then we must assume that your ray is the Sixth. Is yours a mind which wants to prove and plan, to find an exact proof for everything in life?—that is the Fifth Ray at work, the Ray of Science. Does the symbolism of Egypt interest you as a line of approach to God?—then probably it is the Fourth Ray which is guiding and inspiring your work. However, there are many little sub-rays, and only your own intuition and sense will help you to understand the main ray to which you respond.

A young soul may also appear to have the characteristics of one particular ray overdeveloped. This does not happen as such; let us turn it around. If, let us say, a person of the First Ray proves very dominant, this does not mean that he or she should change, that these particular qualities are not good in themselves; rather, it means that other qualities are not yet sufficiently developed to balance out those of the first ray. We must attain to perfect balance. Thus there is one dominant note in the character, but the influence of each ray has to be blended to get perfect attunement. Similarly, you go through three major initiations as you move forward. But there are many minor ones, varying with each soul. One soul will perhaps in one initiation gain as much as another soul in several. But we tell you that we have learnt of three great initiations, through which every soul must some day pass. It is possible for you to get the knowledge of which initiations you have passed, but it will only come to you intuitionally through the Buddhic plane.

To Help Others

Contrary to what you might understand from our teaching, the materialist has his or her place in the grand scheme of evolution. He or she brings to humanity a power, a driving force, which eventually causes the opening of the higher mind. For out of that compelling hunger is born another urge: that of love … love to make contact with something he or she does not understand but nonetheless feels; something which through a slowly awakening intuition, the soul knows he or she needs; something in kinship with him or herself, something attuned to that urge within him or herself for love. This person does not always desire to love, to give love; *but desires to be loved*. From this suppressed flame within us all, is born the desire to understand what is invisible, but can nonetheless be sensed and felt. For the mind tells you, when you look forth upon an awakening spring, when you listen to gentle and grand music, when you wonder at a sunset or the brilliance of the starlit night, that behind these manifestations of beauty there must be a power ... perhaps a mind, an intellect, which has caused all; and the power strikes a harmonious note within your breast. For not only the beauty of colour and form, the majesty of nature, but some vibration invisible and behind the physical manifestation brings harmony to your soul. Some have thus become aware that there exists what is described as a 'spirit world'.

Let us not judge any soul by its simplicity or apparent ignorance on the outer plane. The disciples who gathered to form the early Christian church, the little brotherhood that existed at the beginning, were evolved souls. They had brought into activity those higher bodies of which we were speaking, the intuitional and the spiritual—indeed the celestial bodies. They had had revealed to them certain forms and ceremonies which would put them in touch with a reservoir of power and love and wisdom generated on the higher planes of life for distribution to humanity, to help people on the path of evolution.

Do you know what the world lacks so much? It is the power of imagination. Imagination is vision, and it is a creative power. And where there is no vision, as you know from your Bible, the people perish.[11] Humanity falls down. If you develop the gift of imagination, you can put yourself into the heart of your brother or sister. As soon as this creative power, this light, begins to grow in you, it sends out its feelers like little fine threads through all forms of life. In time you will develop this sense of feeling—this sense of feeling through your imagination and through your desire to serve. Remember the importance of feeling; because through feeling you develop the Christ within. Do not be ashamed of your feelings. They are the pointers, the guides which direct you along the path of light.

When your heart centre opens in love and kindness towards all creatures, it begins to grow and to expand, and can be seen by those with clear vision as a light radiating forth. Love God faithfully, and this light waxes and becomes brighter. By the power of this light miracles can be wrought, healings performed, and all the spiritual beauty of human life is revealed. Development of this kind of sunlight within your own being enables you to develop what is loosely called clairvoyance or clear vision. Clear vision means an inward knowing. When you have this, you know the truth; you recognize the love that exists in your brethren. You also comprehend their soul-needs. If you have not developed the light, you are so often deaf and blind to your brother's or sister's need and to the yearning in his or her heart. With clear vision you have an inward recognition of truth, not only in humanity but also in the scriptures of the great religions. You go right to the mark. You are direct in all your dealings, but are also aware of any hurt which your brother or sister may feel, and so you are careful and tender in action and speech.

Expanded Awareness

When people within the inner schools of teaching were spiritually quickened in ancient days, they possessed knowledge which had been passed to them from their teachers. They knew of a spiritual power, a directing influence. Indeed, they worshipped the sun; not merely because it was the life-giver of the physical life, but because they saw beyond and behind the physical manifestation a spiritual power. They recognized the true origin of the sun. The sun worshippers were neither heathens nor idolaters, but rather knew the spiritual meaning of that physical representation of the light, the illumination, the life-giver of their world.

You know that you live in a world of spirit. If you need little convincing of this truth, it is not because you have received evidence of discarnate beings living on the astral plane, but because you are at one with the spiritual world. Your heart or your intuition is your guide. Reason certainly takes a hand in your deductions, in your conclusions, but the truth speaks in you.

We would have you think of the human soul evolving along the path of spirit, of Christhood, until it becomes at one with the power of the Father–Mother, until it holds all illumination and all glory. When it becomes unlimited in its influence, it becomes an actual creative centre or sun. Is it possible for the finite mind to grasp, or for us to put into language, the inner meaning of this truth?

We cannot clothe the idea in words, but your intuition must follow the path through the Christ to the Sun, comprehending if it can the glory of that centre of life and illumination. Then only will you begin to glimpse what lies before you as a soul. On earth your life seems so infinitesimal, so antlike, and yet so full of infinite possibility.

SECTION TWO
DEVELOPING THE INTUITION

VII

ACCEPTING A HIGHER POWER

Learning to Trust

IN THE PAST, there were what are called mystery schools, where the inner life was revealed to pupils. The schools were prevalent in Egypt and later in Greece; and the great initiate Pythagoras drew many aspiring souls to his school. He taught his pupils by signs and symbols, and through the principles of mathematics, music, vibration and colour. He taught concerning the harmony of the spheres. A pupil has to learn through deep thought about God, through meditating and contemplating all life, all nature; and through spiritual revelation he or she has to learn to interpret the wisdom of God.

Today, if you talked about these things to the man or woman in the street, they might think that you were a little strange in your mind, and might even say it was dangerous to think about them. Why do people think these things dangerous? Because they instinctively know that there is an unknown power in them. It can certainly be dangerous to handle fire or electricity or atomic energy carelessly, but we also remember that these revelations of the secrets of nature are God's gifts to humanity, and it is intended that you should unveil these secrets when you know how to do so without danger. If people had refused to handle the unknown quantity of electricity, you would be living in a very different world today. It is right for you to increase your knowledge, but you need to do so with care and to proceed wisely.

Thus it was that the mystery schools taught the pupils how to proceed by degrees and to advance very wisely and slowly, and at each step they had to pass a test or degree. Each degree was a form of initiation. Never were the pupils allowed to rush forward; and if they did, they came up against a sharp instrument. It is all very well to be eager for knowledge, but patience and caution must accompany the pupil on the path. The opposite can do much harm. At the same time, you must not lag behind when the inner voice is gently urging you forward. You know that these spiritual forces lie within yourself. There is always an intuitive power which tells you that you are spirit, and that there are unknown, untried, undeveloped forces within yourself. Faith and trust in that inner voice will prove to you its constancy and its helpfulness as you tread the path of spiritual development and service.

In the Egyptian mysteries, there were ceremonies through which the candidate passed, which were symbolical of certain soul-experiences. In the temples were subterranean passages through which the candidates had to walk. They symbolized the journey of the soul through the sadness and darkness of physical life. Many, many of us are now walking this probationary path; and we find it hard, do we not? So many dark corners there are, so many unexpected turns, and we know not where we go! Sometimes, even our guides seem to confuse us in what they tell us. There remains but one thing to do, and we want you to apply this to your present material and spiritual life: *keep on, with your whole heart in God's keeping.* You say: 'If only I could see the spirit people, they would help me'. You think that you cannot see; you cannot hear; you believe you walk alone.

The test of old is still the test today. Such tests for initiation gauge the candidate's confidence in God's love … nothing else! You walk the path, confused on every hand, others suspecting or misjudging you … sad yourself, perhaps, for failures which you recognize, and troubled by many problems and sorrows. If you would pass the portals of the first initiation (though it may not be the first of these for you), you are throughout being tested in your absolute confidence in God's love. You must feel that God is good, and that whatever comes leads you to a greater understanding of His–Her love. When that thought is so firmly established that nothing shakes it, nothing clouds your vision, then you will walk, with shining eyes, into the land of light: you will pass through that particular initiation, and expansion of consciousness, or a greater understanding of God will come to you. This is the whole purpose of life ... that an individual shall surrender to God's love, acknowledging the Father as the supreme Spirit; acknowledging the Mother, giver of all good.

But if you are troubled about material problems and would wish to talk with your spirit brethren, enter the Silence, and pray thus: that God's love shall be in your heart. Not that God shall lead you, because God *will* lead you. If you know He–She will lead you and you trust in God, God cannot fail you. He–She is already leading you.

We would here digress for a moment by pointing out that the truth of the Christ teaching, now so familiar, has perhaps lost its power by constant repetition. Conventional readers of the scriptures often miss the esoteric meaning. They will say, 'Yes, we know Christ said, *Love one another*'. They think they are merely bidden to be normally decent and kind when it is easy to be loving and kind. But should these people come up against some big problem where this truth is deeply involved, they then say, 'Oh yes, Christ's teaching is all very well; but we are living in the world and we are forced to do as the world does. You can't allow people to trample upon you; you must stand up for your rights.'

Is this the way, the truth, and the life? Is this really the teaching of Christ? Why can't men and women put his doctrine into practice? *Because they are afraid to trust in the power of love.* Yet love is the dynamic force which brought life to the world. Were this love withdrawn from manifestation on earth, death would ensue.

From these many instances, you will gather that the great and the advanced soul will hold fast to that inner consciousness that God is good. God visits apparent sufferings upon His–Her children out of love, because only through these events can the soul gain strength, only through these experiences can the soul learn to stand unmoved.

My brethren, as we talk, you can feel that inner poise come: that inner strength which inspires in you the greatest courage. You know that nothing, *no thing*, has power to destroy that eternal love, that living flame, within. Nothing matters, literally *nothing* matters much so long as you know God or Christ within you.

Meditation and Trust

But there is a great deal for each of you to overcome. For instance, as you progress on the spiritual path, you are also increasing your sensitivity; the nervous system becomes very sensitive. You tread a very narrow path. On the one hand, you need to develop this sensitivity—because this is the quality which enables you to receive heavenly guidance and comfort and help in your daily life. On the other hand, you also have to develop the inner power of God, which brings tranquillity. This power of God is love. The soul who has developed true love also acquires wisdom. The soul developing tranquillity achieves the quality of God's peace. When the soul can touch that degree of tranquillity which brings humility, then its eyes are opened and it sees far beyond the limitations of the ordinary physical mind.

So, to comprehend spiritual truth and divine law, a person must strive to follow the guidance of his or her inner light. He or she must not only obey the voice of God within, but must trust that voice; and even if the individual sometimes feels restive under the experiences which come, he or she must keep faith. Humanity needs faith in and obedience to the voice of God within, and you need to have faith in that divine guiding light which is working through you. When you have achieved these virtues, you no longer question with your earthly mind the wisdom of God's laws. You are able then to surrender to the love of God. You are able to accept, accept, *accept*.

Against this, the earthly mind will pop up again and say, 'But surely I should accept nothing against my reason. God (if there be a God) has given me that reason'. How true! But the true reason, the real reasoning power in a person, can always be satisfied by spiritual light. When light dawns in your heart, when through your own experience you have been drawn close to the heart of God or the Master, you both see and know. You do not then need books to tell you, nor yet anyone speaking as we are speaking to you. Your very experience in meditation, or in a state of contemplation or prayer, gives you something which can never be described;

but in this experience, which is communion with your Creator, you know truth.

If you are going on a journey to a distant country, usually you will make some effort to find out as much as you can about that country. You will probably obtain maps and guidebooks for your journey. These will help you by giving you helpful directions on how to reach your destination and describing the country to which you are going. Beyond that they can do nothing. They cannot provide you with the means of transport; they cannot travel for you. You have actually to travel, to experience for yourself; and through that experience you learn so much more than you can ever learn from reading maps and guidebooks. What we are trying to make plain is that when you are quickened in spirit, knowing that you have come from afar and are embarked on a long journey, then you are ready to experience all the beauty laid out before you and all around you. You are able to experience the joy of your physical state; you are able to breathe in, in fuller consciousness, the divine life-forces. You must experience every detail of life with all your senses—with your physical, your mental and your spiritual senses.

Now one of the greatest helps to you on your journey in search of God (and this is the purpose of this life) is meditation. Books will not get you there, although they can point the way; words will not get you there. You have to take the journey yourself. You have to experience for yourself those higher states of consciousness, the reality of the inner world. This can begin for you in the practice of meditation. With your first contact with the universal life, through meditation, something happens to you which has never happened before.

Many of you, in your early experience of meditation, have been disappointed and felt that you were getting nowhere. You saw nothing; you heard nothing; it just seemed as though you were sitting in darkness—but not quite, because occasionally you might have seen or imagined a colour; or you might have imagined something but you would not trust yourself. You said, 'Oh, I don't think it was true; it was all in my mind'. But what you have to remember is that spiritual truth and awareness is the greatest gift of God to humanity, and so this gift has to be patiently sought. If it were easy to find that state of indescribable joy, why, all the world would be there already.

Here is a thought for you: in your state of meditation, of tranquillity, you are alone … with God.

VIII

STAGES OF DEVELOPMENT

Development of Body, Soul and Spirit

ON THE PATH of spiritual unfoldment, we must recognize three distinct paths which mainly run in sequence, and yet at times overlap each other. First comes the training and preparation of the physical body; next, the training and preparation of the soul; and lastly, the training and the discipline and awakening of the spirit.

Tests

Once we have arrived at that point on the path where initiation begins, we shall find tests in preparation for this initiation on each one of these planes—body, soul and spirit. We always advise moderation, and gentle development, but there are certain truths necessary for us to recognize in our training for initiation.

The elements composing the body must be purified if the soul and the spirit are to be quickened to receive impression and inspiration from their true home. If the body is coarsened by the gratification of animal desires, such coarseness must form a barrier, preventing the expansion of the soul and the illumination of the mind by the spirit. The attitude of mind towards food should be that of thankfulness for the blessing of pure food. Commonsense must be brought to bear. Never force the body to abstain from food that is actually necessary for some particular job in hand. For instance, many people are compelled to live a life of hardship. If they work very hard, physically, their bodies need food that is different from those of people who are able to choose what they do and choose the vibrations they surround themselves with. If life is hard and rough, the difficulties are given for a purpose, and means that there are lessons to be learnt through such a condition. The soul aspiring on the path accepts that condition, recognizing it as necessary for his or her development. On the other hand, we must remember that the physical body is the temple which houses the Holy Spirit.

As the soul develops, as its vibrations become more subtle, we meet with perhaps the first and greatest test—that of *dispassion*. The soul is by nature emotional, and easily becomes indignant, upset, and hurt by trifling things. To become dispassionate, we think, is one of the most important lessons; and it is a statement which bears repetition. *The soul must learn to keep its equilibrium and not get unduly upset.* Do not fly into a rage because something does not please you, or because someone has hurt you. Do not give way to depression when things go wrong, but instead endeavour to attain and maintain an even and still vibration.

Many other subtle lessons come to test and try would-be aspirants on the path. You are tested for fear. You are also tested for discrimination, and as you all follow the path, many of you indeed fall on that stile. You find you cannot discriminate between good and evil, between the false and the true. In some situations, you find that you do not even understand what good and evil are. But these lessons have to be learned. If your soul comes up against a certain experience which it would do anything to escape from or alter, and if the lesson proves very hard to bear, then make it your aim to go through with a patient and steady spirit. Know that it is perhaps karma that has to be endured, and that in doing so you are paying off a past debt. More than this, you are being given an opportunity to learn the lesson of dispassion. However difficult that human experience may prove, it will be worthwhile.

One other point of the utmost importance on the spiritual path is that of avoiding spiritual pride. How often did the master Jesus stress that lesson throughout His ministry? Again and again he laid bear the hypocrisy of groups such as the Pharisees of his time. This same lesson is one bound to confront every soul, and it comes in many subtle forms. The soul setting forth upon the path of spiritual aspiration can make so much progress that it becomes inflated with its own spiritual grandeur and power. Having set out with a pure desire to serve humanity, and having advanced to a certain extent along the path, it begins to feel that it is a fine person, and doing a magnificent work. Then comes the test. That soul has to face an unexpected test of its spiritual reality and truth, and its spiritual humility. How will it respond?

As you can see, it is very important for children to be instructed in spiritual knowledge, so that they may learn at an early age to control temper, to treat animals kindly, to have love and tenderness for their child companions. It is important for them to learn how to tend and grow flowers, because knowledge comes in due course which will give them greater power to help nature and the animal kingdoms, to commune with the angelic. The soul may learn from the angels some of the secrets of nature—such as the secret of the wind-currents, and of the heavenly constellations and the influence they bear upon life on earth. Mastership means that the spirit of a person must be master, must control the lower planes of life. It must be master of the physical body, and of the emotional and mental. The spirit must attain complete power and direction over the lower vehicles. As a captain commands the ship, so must the master hold supreme control over his or her body and soul.

A soul is never overlooked when it is ready for initiation into the great Light. So when a measure of control has been learned, and when these earthly tests have been safely passed, the time comes for that soul to be summoned into the great Hall of Initiation. When initiation comes, there will be powers bestowed upon the aspirant—powers on the physical plane, giving strength and endurance; powers given to the soul and the mind. Great illumination and power will come to the spirit.

Raising the Consciousness every Day

One more point, of great value, concerns the training you undergo in meditation. Do not overdo, but do not neglect the daily meditation. If you can only set aside ten minutes in the morning and at night, or even less—try never to fail in this daily contact with the eternal source of light and truth. This daily meditation is a training for the body, a training in self-control, making it do whatever your spirit desires. It is training in not letting it have its own way. The daily meditation also gives training in control of the soul and mind, and training in the directing power of the spirit.

St Paul said that there is a terrestrial body and a celestial body.[12] With the first, you touch, see, smell and feel terrestrial things; with the second, you contact celestial states of life. Do not think in terms of here on earth and there in heaven, but know that you have bodies with which to contact all worlds. Within you has been implanted the seed of the Christ-being. In the process of your spiritual development this Christ-being will elevate the whole of your own being; you will expand your consciousness, your aura, the atmosphere immediately around you, to reach those most beautiful planes. It is an expansion of consciousness at will and a withdrawal from that expansion at will, a rhythmic inbreathing and outbreathing of life.

Do not therefore be ashamed of your feelings. Be glad that you can feel or sense more spiritual states. But at the same time, remember your need to control and purify the feelings. As we have said, the whole act of spiritual evolution is a purification of the lower atoms and the elements of all life, until the fabric of the earth itself becomes so purified that to the cruder states of life it will become invisible. To you, in your present state of life, the higher worlds are invisible, simply because you have not reached the stage in your evolution when your atoms are purified and your vibrations quickened so that you are attuned to the more spiritual states.

You must seek God within your heart. Until God is active in your heart, you cannot recognize God anywhere. You may not call the yearning within you 'God', but all that is good, true, beautiful and loving in you springs from God. We want now to draw you all up into those celestial spheres. We want you to feel in your deepest soul, in the great Silence, the Source of your life, God, deep within you....

Beloved brethren, if we seem to be grave, it does not mean that we are sombre. Rather, would we raise all present to the heights, for we are encircled by radiant ones. The golden circle of the Christ love is around us and those from the unseen world come to raise the vibrations to spheres of wisdom and light. We remember this as we open our consciousness to the ministering angels. We are taught by them not merely through words but through the language of the spirit. A bridge between the higher worlds and the earth is built and angels cross this bridge to you. Yet they can only cross it when you also ascend to the mountain top—in other words, when you raise your consciousness so that the higher mind becomes receptive and absorbs spiritual truth and wisdom.

Steps

There are three major steps into the mystery schools The first degree is that of the student, the learner. When the feet are set on the path and the desire to learn becomes urgent, the student attracts the attention of the great Lords of Karma; the student is saying: 'I want knowledge; I want to grow; I want to be of use to God and to the Masters. Make me worthy, O God, to be Thy servant!' Then comes the process of purification. Let us remember that the higher vehicles of an individual need much cleansing. The invisible vehicles need purification, along with the physical, because much has been gathered into them which hinders and obstructs. Frequently, therefore, trouble, sickness, suffering then comes into the life-passage of the student. One soul may be born disabled; another may endure great tragedy; a third, possibly, commit crime. Seeing beneath the surface, we always see the working-out of karma in the sorrows of humanity. We know that this or that soul takes suffering and degradation to itself because it needs to be purged of conditions which were brought about in a previous incarnation. We would remind you that suffering and sorrow, along with separation from loved ones, may be your own choice. It may be karma which the highest part of you has selected: taken on so that you could be prepared, purified, made ready for initiation.

The next step—the second degree—is that of the disciple. The disciple must learn obedience, implicit obedience to the master of wisdom and truth. The disciple learns to be exact and precise in all his or her working. No slipshod methods about the disciple! The individual works with his or her 'tools' upon the lower self, shaping and perfecting it. He or she follows the Master, Christ, within his or her own breast (we do not simply mean the Christian Jesus), and the master of wisdom who teaches wisdom and the way of life associated with it. Absolute truth and honesty, then, is demanded of the disciple. No deception!

The third degree begins when the disciple is ready to receive illumination, when he or she can be trusted to receive the secrets of heaven; when, in other words, the individual is able to come into the presence of the Most High … an initiate. He or she must be able to function on the invisible planes freely, for true initiation only takes place in these higher planes; the initiate is a soul touched by the Master's hand and raised to a sublime degree. The initiated being is one born again from the grave of materialism and illusion—the grave of earth; one born again into the true light of his or her heavenly home. Initiation takes place on the invisible planes of life, and the initiate is then at one with their Brothers and Sisters in the grand school or the Great White Lodge.

Nowadays, you may be your own mystery school. Every daily experience, every relationship with your companion beings, will reveal, if you look for it, hidden mystery. You do not need to read books, you only need to love, to be still within, and be patient, to meditate, to observe—and then the mystery school within the temple of your own being will teach all that you need to know. You may read, if you like, but do not let books be your props. If you find them interesting, take and read and ponder. But it is not necessary. We can think of many who are full of profound wisdom, inner wisdom, and yet never read a book. The master Jesus, according to the gospel story, did not spend his time reading books; during those three years of his ministry he took for his lessons the simple things of everyday life and used them for his teaching. He says to you now, '*What I can do, you can do also*'.[13]

IX

HEART WORK

Beauty, the Principle of the Seventh (the Violet) Ray

WE HAVE spoken of the higher world as the invisible world, only because you cannot see it from your own level of life. In the invisible universe are the most wonderful, beautiful things. We cannot tell you of them, or describe them, simply because you do not have, yet, even a capacity to imagine these things. Imagination is really the power of the Creator working in you. You visualize, or you create an image. That image can only be representative of the degree of development of the God within you.

Then of course you must remember that there are so many aspects of beauty. Only a truly infinitesimal part of the glory of God's creation is visible until you have unfolded and developed the spiritual powers to see, which means to create. Within every one of you, however young or old, lies this life, this power, this God within.

You all have much to hope for, to bring forth from your innermost self. You have power within you to develop vision and understanding of all these glories. Access to these spheres, these planes, these levels of life—from the physical to the dense etheric, the astral, the mental, the higher mental and the celestial, and even beyond—is already within you; but you have to find the key and earn knowledge of how to unlock the particular gate leading to them.

We would describe to you a lovely pink rose which is opening its petals to the sun. A rose is the symbol of a human heart, fragrant with love. With this symbol before you, be very still, be at peace…. At this celestial level of consciousness, you should develop the power to receive truth, the power of feeling and imagination. If you feel the beauty of the heaven worlds, you are receiving divine truth intuitively. This is how you can discriminate between God's will and self-will. The disciple leaves all earthly things—mind, body, possessions, desires—to follow the Master. 'Leave all and follow me,' said Jesus. Having reached this understanding, you can safely rely upon your intuition. It all comes to these few simple words: 'Be still and know that I am God'. Be still … in love, and know that *I am.*

God's plan is to bring beauty—we will not say perfection, not in the limited sense in which the word is understood. To us there is no standing still; even with God—we do not see a Being utterly perfected, completely finished and there for ever…. Instead, we wonder at and worship a God ever growing more beautiful, ever sending forth greater waves of life and light, expressing Himself–Herself: not only in this universe, but in universes yet unborn.

In the Aquarian Age, the intuition of children will be unfolded as they learn, and it will be stimulated with vibrations of beauty, of colour, and art and form. The ear will be trained to hear beautiful music, the eye to see beauty. There will be beauty expressed throughout life; beauty … the external expression of the spirit: beauty, not the creation of intellect alone, but in itself an expression of the Divine.

The spirit must remain unaffected by the challenge—that is the word we will use—the challenge of matter, of the lower life. Strive to respond to beauty and strive to feel love towards all life. Let your heart be always in tune with the Infinite Love. If you can live in this manner, you will be living your meditation.

We repeat that not one of you can have any conception at present of the beauty which lies before you. All we can say is: 'Ask, and ye shall receive; seek, and ye shall find (find exactly what you are in truth seeking); and knock (live right action and right thought), and you will be admitted into the Temple of the Holy Mysteries, where the glories of the heaven world await you. And there you will find that complete at-one-ment with the Divine Spirit, God, your Creator.[14] Yet even beyond this, there is still advancement; for God is not static. Remember, God can never be static when all life is ever demonstrating growth, movement and progress. Can you ever come to an end? No, indeed! Nor is there any such thing as a straight line; it must curve and join at the end and make a circle. So therefore your life goes on and on: never wearying, never disappointing, but ever unfolding and progressing, because God takes you onward with Him–Her, and is ever growing, expanding and reaching higher to a more glorious life.

Healing

The practice of the presence of the Christ within you is doing more than creating pleasant spiritual experiences. It is helping you to build healthy soul bodies and healthy physical bodies for your habitation in many lives to come. All the time you are creating the vehicles—physical, etheric, emotional, mental and celestial—for the future.

There are many spheres, many states of life for the child of God to experience. But you cannot see a beautiful picture if you are blind, and you cannot smell a lovely flower if you have no sense of smell. You cannot hear the music of the spheres if you are deaf to them. Therefore, you must develop the faculties which will enable you—a divine soul, a divine spirit—to experience the glories of all those other spheres of life which are your inheritance.

We do not like to emphasize too much the effect which violent emotion has upon physical health, but we must speak the truth. There is nothing which causes a more severe reaction on the physical body. You may not always recognize it as a cause of dis-ease. You may suffer bodily pain and put it down to some physical origin. But on the path the aspirant must be prepared to acknowledge truth. Emotions which shake not only the physical but all the inner bodies eventually cause some kind of physical upheaval which will manifest in a minor or major degree. Therefore, control of the emotional body and the transmutation of all the lower passions into the higher, so that you give forth love and constructive power instead of hate and destructive power, is certain to have an enormously beneficial effect.

The Great White Light of Christ is the healer of all ills of body and of soul. It heals the physical body, and is the great dissolver of all shadows. It is ever the builder, ever the constructor; and you are called by the hosts invisible into service with the light, into action.

We hear from you the question, 'how can we serve, how act?'. You must endeavour to *become aware* of the invisible forces which are playing upon the earth life. You must train your body and your higher vehicles to become consciously aware of this stream of light which finds entrance into your being through the psychic centres. You must learn to be aware of this circulating light stream which vivifies and can glorify body and soul. It can pass from you, directed by your highest self, to heal the sick throughout the world, whether they are sick in body or in mind.

The vibrations and the power of the angels and the great spiritual beings work through human channels to build heaven into the *consciousness* of humanity. This is the Ancient Wisdom (that is, the temple training of the past) ... training in becoming aware of the land of light, of the light within the soul; of the effect of colour upon the soul, upon the mind, upon the body ... the effect of perfume ... the effect of sound.

Remember, as you open yourself, that you are a channel for the light and power of the masters. As you give from your very soul in healing, so you grow in wisdom, intelligence, intuition, perception. Take notice of the changing vibrations in your own body as you progress with your healing. He who has so much of this healing work in His care is the Master Jesus, who was and still is the channel for the Great Light, this world life-force, even the Christ Spirit.

Opening up the Heart

Without waiting for any special moment to do this, try to visualize a great white hall, and the golden rays of wisdom pouring through the canopy of heaven upon you. You are at one with a multitude, a grand company of souls present, both human and angelic. White Eagle, we say, is merely the instrument in this spirit world, and not of himself does he speak. The golden light of wisdom can pour through the heart of any son or daughter of God, and all are sons and daughters of God.

Thus in your own home, within your inner sanctuary, perhaps among this grand company, you may be both listener and teacher. This is a profound inner truth—that you can at the same time listen and teach. Even a master can be at the same time a pupil; and it is precisely because he or she can realize that he or she is ever a pupil, that such a one attains to mastership.

Whoever may listen is a pupil listening to the master; but the master's teaching comes through your heart, the mind in your heart, and not through the mind of the head. You will understand this better when you ponder the words of Jesus, *Except you become as a little child, you cannot enter into the kingdom.* To become a little child means that there must be a transference from the thinking which you do in the brain to feeling and intuition in the heart centre. Then the spirit of humility in your heart, like the little child, will listen; and it will also teach the mind in the head. Does not your Bible say, *A little child shall lead them?*[15] All such sayings, although they can apply to the outer world, and to happenings on the outer plane, have an esoteric meaning—they come from within and radiate to what is outside. So from within the heart the truth can radiate and manifest in simple childlike kindliness and love on the physical plane of life. Thus a little child shall lead them: Christ, the Child which resides in the centre of the heart. This heart centre, we tell you, is the centre of your universe.

When you think in the ordinary way, you do so with

your mind operating through the brain. The brain is a wonderful organism, and it is not only physical but has an etheric counterpart. Even now, as you read, it is your head centre or brain interpreting our words. You are thinking with your brain. Many people make the mistake of accepting the brain as the only reliable receiving-station for truth. The head centre can play an important part in the spiritual development of a person; but there is also, as we have said, a mind in the heart centre.

The heart, too, is a very wonderful organ, with many more aspects than medical science has discovered. It too has an etheric counterpart which plays an important part in the birth, growth, life, and death of the physical body. We refer not so much to the actual heart, which appears to be placed slightly towards the left of the body, as to the heart centre or chakra. That is the spiritual counterpart of the physical heart, and it is right in the centre of the breast. Its location is at the thymus gland, much as at the head centre we have the pineal and pituitary glands. In spiritual development, then, even though the head plays a part in the early days when a person is beginning to become aware of spiritual worlds around him or her and the spiritual life, the person at that stage can only know through his or her mind. Later on, when that individual contacts the heavenly light, a change takes place and the mind of the heart begins to function.

Let us try explain it yet another way. There are

many brilliant men and women—great students with knowledge and wonderful mental apparatus, able to express themselves through speech and pen without a flaw. But within the heart they may know nothing. The heart within may be like a stone. Not that they are necessarily unkind or cruel. The heart within a brilliant intellectual may on some occasions be like a dead thing which has never been awakened. This you recognize when great human sorrow touches that person; and he or she is impotent to deal with it. Nothing can give the individual the answer to life's problems. The intellect, the mind, when it comes to the major experiences of life—birth, sickness, joy, life, death—cannot explain or answer anything.

The heart centre, or mind in the heart, is like the castle in the fairy story, all overgrown with vines and ivy and undergrowth. Within the castle, the beautiful princess sleeps through the centuries until the Prince of Love breaks in, kisses her, and brings her back to life. Such old stories are full of profound mystical and occult teaching.

At the same moment as the soul of a person commences in manifestation, so does the mind in the heart commence to function. The heart mind grows as soon as you learn to *be*, instead of the mind thinking. Yet the mental person apparently knows everything! He or she can explain theology, and grasp all the religions of the past and present; and yet find them empty. They mean nothing unless the mind of the heart is functioning.

The learning gleaned from books and facts must be enriched by human kindliness.

For each individual truly to become part of the great universe of God, that heart centre has to grow, radiate affection, burn as a great fire in the individual soul. The soul has to live, not for itself and its own glorification, but to serve and minister to people, healing the sick and comforting the sorrowful, feeding the hungry. An individual's religion must express itself in practical service on earth. Then, indeed, the heart mind is functioning.

Everyone is a universe in him or herself. Just how wonderful this truth is, none yet comprehends. The individual, the microcosm, is a universe; and the centre or the sun of that universe is the heart—not the head. As the sun is the central point for your solar system, so your heart is the centre of your universe. As the sun works in conjunction with the seven planets, so the heart is receiving the rays, or the influence, of the selfsame planets which cast their rays upon the earth. Some astrologers say that the heart is ruled by the sun. The spiritual counterpart of the physical sun is the Christ Light; when that also is awakened in the heart, the heart-mind commences to function. The physical sun rules the physical heavens, and Christ rules through the sun, or the heart of a person, the destiny of humanity and of the earth. The master in the heart must rule the lodge. By this we mean the temple of a man's or woman's being. If the master is not strong enough to control his or her lodge, if there are ruffians who overpower the master, then there is chaos, sickness, unhappiness, darkness. The light has gone out and in the lodge there is no joy, no happiness, no wisdom and no beauty. The master within must rule the lodge of the human heart, controlling every limb and every organ. Then there will be perfect harmony, perfect health. If the heart be cold and dead, then the person is lifeless, has no animation, no warmth, no radiance.

You will understand from all we say how important it is to cultivate your inner life through meditation. This does not mean to sit for hours and hours and think upon your self, but rather to meditate as you go about the world, not letting the head brain be always uppermost. Sometimes in the country, when walking through the lanes, endeavour to become in tune with the eternal life behind the manifestation of trees and flowers. Meditate upon the grandeur and glory of God's universe, so that the heart becomes active. So live that you are not always thinking of trivial things. Do not fill the mind of the head with a lot of trash, but let it be consciously engaged. When you sit at home quietly, let your heart meditate upon beautiful and joyous and helpful things. 'How can I best serve my brother or sister?', you may for instance wonder. You can serve best by understanding them, by helping them, by being kind and thoughtful, by being on the lookout for little ways in which you can be courteous and kindly. Thus the mind in the heart must become active, glorifying God.

X

BEYOND THOUGHT AND EMOTION

Control of the Mind and Thought

WHEN YOU meditate or pray, one of the best ways to prevent the intrusion of the daily mind is to treat the intruder with contempt. Ignore it. Concentrate more strength than ever upon the God within; and that concentration will become so absorbing and so powerful that the little outer mind will retreat, unable to overcome or penetrate the enormous battery of prayer to God. Do not worry about turning out the culprits. Just ignore them. Concentrate with all your strength and all your being upon God. Your concentration possesses you and fills you with power and light; everything else falls away and you become a living battery, a force of divine light.

Similarly, every time a destructive thought comes into your mind in your everyday life, dismiss it at once. You may not recognize it, but this accumulation of destructive thought in the mental body of human kind eventually turns into ideas which create destructive weapons. Instead, you can so easily discipline yourselves to think and create forms of goodness, beauty and harmony.

It is just the same in dealing with the people around you. When you have little difficulties, it is far better to ignore and let them pass; concentrate on the power and strength of Christ within, and these foolish difficulties will disappear. Too much time is wasted on fussing and worrying about little details in your interpersonal relationships. Concentrate on God and the expression of the Christ within. Nothing else matters. You make mountains out of molehills. Remember, *Vengeance is Mine, I will repay, saith the Lord*.[16] When you feel inclined to retaliate because you have suffered an injustice, don't—you can safely leave the working of the law of God to its originator. Justice will be enforced to the uttermost. It is the law.

Concentrate on God; nothing matters in life so much as this, because by concentrating on God and awakening the true faculties of your higher self you are doing all good. You are putting forth every effort in the finest and the truest way in life and on the earth plane. You need not bother about negative things. They automatically right themselves if you get to the centre of truth and God ... power, love, and knowledge.

The human soul has a freewill choice. Although it has to accept certain experiences which the angels of suffering are urging upon it, the soul also can respond to the angels of love. So the human soul, while it must experience suffering and sometimes pain and degradation, has always a good angel near to whisper, 'God is love. Look up my brother, all is well! God enfolds you in His–Her love.' Thus in the midst of all human suffering is that little voice to which all can if they wish respond, which says, 'Hope, my sister; good will come out of this experience'. Look up, love God, love your Master and Christ. This is the freewill choice of everyone, this is the voice of Christ within that speaks. But remember also that no soul can escape experience that the angels of darkness will bring.

And so we want you to remember the words from your Bible: *Whatsoever things are true, whatsoever things are honest, whatsoever things are just, whatsoever things are pure, whatsoever things are lovely, whatsoever things are of good report … think on these things.*[17] Think good thoughts. Think God thoughts. You know it is a very wonderful gift that your Creator has given to you—the power to think, and the power to choose what you think. If you think God thoughts, you are not only sending them out into the world, but you are opening yourself to the inflow of more and more wisdom, heavenly wisdom. You are raising the vibration of all humanity; and as you do this you are developing your sensitivity—your power of clear vision and clear hearing, and your power of healing.

Blending Intellect and Feeling

What is an individual's protection, then, against the negative influences which surround the earth plane? A pure heart, pure loving aspirations, we would say. Your desires then are not of the lower nature, but of the true Self, the Christ within. The true self seeks to serve, and takes no thought for itself. It indeed has no time to think of its own progress, its own initiations, of that splendid moment when it will at last enter the Great White Lodge. It thinks not of these, but of how it can best serve and love those whom God sends within its orbit. Service, through love, is the focus of the true self.

How necessary it is to distinguish between love, which is wisdom, and emotionalism, which may disintegrate love! How necessary to recognize a love seeking not its own, opening wide its heart, thinking not harshly of that denomination or that sect, this sinner or that, not condemning, but accepting that in all planes the great scheme of God develops! Such love accepts that even in so-called 'evil' there is a purpose, for that which is called 'evil' in people's hearts is ever used by the Omnipotent to teach, through experience and through suffering, through the lesson of the cross to the moment of dawn, that people may see the sun rising upon the new age.

When carried away by joy or overwrought by pain,[18] or at any time when you are emotionally over-stressed, you are like a frail boat tossed about in a storm. Yet within everyone awaits the sleeping Master, the indwelling Christ. When at last you can call upon Him in your distress, crying, 'Master, help me!' you are appealing not to any outside teacher but to the Christ within. You cry, 'O Thou who art light and power and love, come to my aid!' Then tranquillity steals over you. You are at last aware of an indwelling strength and you become still. Perhaps later, when you have trained yourself in meditation, you can feel yourself rise as on a shaft of light at this time. You then have power to function on a plane superior to this one and, looking down upon your emotional disturbance, you will see it for what it really is.

This control over emotion, anger and fear is one of the earliest degrees of initiation. It is achieved not by repression but by sublimation of these emotions, which can be seen by the clairvoyant as tongues of flame darting through the aura. All such things can be subdued and transmuted by the Christ within, and any passion that has been aroused, instead of injuring and destroying—for it *can* destroy—goes forth instead with power to heal, to bless, to lighten the burdens of the world, manifesting amid the darkness as pure white light.

Yes, it is said that one of the greatest barriers for a soul on the path is to overcome violent emotion, by which we mean to transmute it. Let it come out, but let it come out in love and as a cool, peaceful, harmonious vibration.

The Test of Still Water

'Know thyself, and thou shalt know God and the universe.… Be still … and know God.' Sometimes people in your so-called advanced civilization ask why, with their great intellects, they should be asked to learn from the North American Indian guides? It is because your Indian brethren learned to draw aside from the world; to climb the heights; to dwell in the silence. It is because they lived by the running water and heard the song of the wind in the trees and took to themselves the companionship of nature. It is because they heard the voice of God speak within the silence. Thus intellect was changed into intelligence, and with intelligence came power and perfection.

Be still, and know God, and thou shalt possess abundance of all things.

In meditation, coming from the harsh and turbulent conditions of earth, the soul on entering the higher planes needs to be purified before it can proceed further, and so it is thus cleansed.

You know that by the water initiation is meant the training of the emotional body. Water denotes the psychic and the emotional, and so those who pass the water initiation have learned about psychic things and emotions and have learned to discriminate between the real and the unreal. They have learned to balance the emotions so that these do not stand in the way of the activity of the spirit or the Christ within. It has been said that dispassion is one of the hardest lessons for the neophyte to learn. It is so easy to be stirred and emotionally upset by contact with inharmonious conditions. But as the Christ light within grows stronger it teaches the neophyte to control passion and emotion, to keep it stilled and in its right place, so that emotion can be used for spiritual service but is not allowed to storm through the soul, upsetting and shattering all its spiritual vibrations.

So we learn through the water initiation the meaning of being *still*, when the soul may know tranquillity and God under all conditions. The neophyte is calm but not indifferent: there is a difference between indifference and lethargy on the one hand and tranquillity and calmness based on strength on the other. In the latter condition, a clear perspective is attained and the soul is directed by the Master, the Christ.

XI

BECOMING STILL

Being the Christ Within

MEDITATION and union with God is of the utmost value in daily life. It is better to *be* good than to dissipate energy in an endeavour to *do* good. Being good, being God-conscious, being God-loving, being God-wise, does far more to help life than misplaced energy which is trying to do good. Therefore choose being, rather than seeming to be.

Many of you have come back into incarnation not to enjoy yourself but because you want to help humanity. This may not necessarily be by going to meetings or doing good works, but because your very presence in life can be a joy and comfort to those about you: to the family into which you are born, and to the family of which you are the parent. You can serve best not by scattering your energies and forces but by *being a child of God* and giving warmth and light—to help every flower bloom its best in the particular patch or garden in which you find yourself.[19]

So we love God. We raise our thoughts to the apex of the Golden Triangle and visualize there the glorious

Star. We hold that Star, that point of light; and in that point of light, right in the centre of that perfect geometrical six-pointed Star, we may hold the image of anyone we desire to help. Or we may just hold the Star and see the rays raying forth. If you do this properly and in sincerity, in truth and in belief that what we tell you is true, you will succeed not only in helping your patients, helping the world by sending out light into the darkness of matter, but you will at the same time be developing within yourself that lovely Golden Flower and be living in the Star Temple.

This is the secret: To live, to know and *to be*, to be in the consciousness of the Infinite Love and Light, and to live for spirit and not for matter. Matter is secondary; spirit is the first and foremost aspect of a human being, and to live rightly you must live to develop the consciousness of the Great White Light or the Christ within yourself. Not in the brow, my friends, but in the heart, and in the thousand-petalled lotus at the apex of your triangle.

Work always with this higher triangle, and the Star. The triangle is in the Star—your triangle on its base, and the balancing triangle of your higher self penetrating, coming down to unite and form the Star.... You are in it, and you have to become aware that you are in it, and you have to develop the consciousness of the power of this Star to perform miracles. But remember it is not your will when a miracle is performed. It is God's power; it is God's will. Only God works miracles.

God is the light in humanity, and God alone gives or withdraws according to His–Her wisdom. We hope you understand that and will not force what you think ought to be done. Surrender, my children, surrender to God's will in all things.

Accept, knowing that God is wise in giving, and wiser still in taking away. The whole point is that as the soul evolves and expands in God-consciousness, it cannot really lose anything. For then it knows that nothing is lost in God's creation. Only a limited consciousness prevents that soul from recognizing that *all is here, all is present*. There is no separation when you become conscious of the world of spirit, when you can expand your consciousness beyond the limitations of the mortal mind and brain.

Surrender

You speak of peace, you pray for peace, you seek peace on earth. The way to realize this ideal is to live in tranquillity yourself. To attain this tranquillity of spirit, surrender life and all it means to God; surrender all anxiety and fear and irritation to God; then the balm of tranquillity flows into the soul, and you are at peace.

This is what we mean when we point to the Cross of Light. For the soul who would receive that cross, who would bear that cross within his or her heart, must have learnt the lesson of discrimination and surrender … surrender of the lower self to the Divine. So you see what the surrender means ... what the sacrifice of the cross means? It is not easy. It sounds easy, perhaps; looks easy on paper: but when it comes to putting it into action in everyday life, it is one of the hardest lessons that you have to learn.

And so we associate the symbol of the cross with humility, with surrender. We recall another symbolic interpretation—the 'laying down' of all that life on earth holds most dear. In very truth, the things of the desire body must be laid aside, the desires of earth overcome! Crucifixion means to us the opening of the temple door ... of heaven itself ... of light eternal. *Only when you lay down life can you hope to find life!* Have you not heard these words before, and have they remained merely words? Words pointing your thoughts to the death of the physical body? No, indeed; it does not refer to bodily death, but to the death or laying down of the desire body, the lower self; the setting of all earthly desires in abeyance, so that the Christ within may reign.

Must we then go through life without thought or care for the necessities of the body and of life about us? No. Rather, these must take a subsidiary place; they may not tempt nor urge the soul to seek only for itself, without thought for the whole.

When a soul has given its heart, itself, to the Master; when it has seen the path of initiation, and is therefore a disciple of the Master, nothing happens to that disciple which is not in the plan. This may be a very difficult point for many to accept. They feel they may go wrong, and through stupidity make some false step. 'Where is freewill in this', they ask, 'if all that a disciple passes through falls into the plan?' And we tell you, it is because a disciple, at that stage, does not know self-will. Do you not see? The disciple has surrendered his or her will utterly and completely to God. A disciple knows, or learns, that all is the working out of the law. By stepping onto the path, he or she is saying: 'I am ready for anything; I have one object, and that is to progress as steadily as possible, to gain and absorb wisdom, love and power from God. Not for myself alone, but that in so doing I may help my companions on the path'. The disciple thinks not in terms of self alone, but views life as a whole. It is no longer 'I'; it is 'my brethren'.

We would stress the point that nothing happens outside the plan. We mean, there is no question; the disciple knows that the things which come are all for the good. See good always; know that good is coming out of the difficulties in which you find yourself. We stress this point, because we know there are some who are suffering through a karmic condition which they have decided to wade through. You will get through … you will get through. Do not lose your vision that God is good: 'Not what I want, but what Thou wantest, O God'.

Overcoming Fear

Your heart must know, as you tune into the higher self on the violet ray, that all fear is unnecessary. Fear is disintegrating. It breaks down the power of the light; it causes havoc in your body, in your bloodstream, in your nervous system. It is a waster. You know better than to fear, but we do recognize the difficulties under which you labour. One of them is that the mass of humanity is constantly exuding fear thoughts. Etherically, all these go forth as a nasty grey, or are even brown or black in hue. It is for you to surround yourself not with them but with positive thought, with light that your yourself project from your heart centre. You can let that Star in your heart and head shine forth in full power, and its very light will encompass and protect you. Instead of allowing your aura to be impinged upon by the murky colours, you can send forth from within colours of beauty and brightness, so as to dispel the dark clouds around the earth.

The natural instinct for self-preservation is of the lower self, not of the higher. The higher self has to learn to command and to impress upon the lower self that all is well. All fear must be overcome. This is one of the greatest tests. Often, we tell you there is nothing to fear in life except fear. And if you examine yourself, we are sure you will realize fear to be one of the greatest foes. Fear of hurt, fear of what is going to happen in material life, fear of death … fear of all kinds. Fear must be transmuted to love and trust.

The difficult part is for a soul to live, day by day, in a dark world, absorbing the lessons which the outer life is intended to teach. If you persevere with the one small lesson, which is to cast out fear, for even just a few weeks, at the end of that time you will realize what a great step forward you have taken. Be without fear. Surrender to God. You will be filled with love and light; you will help the world forward towards peace, and will help all those who are in darkness because they are full of fear—even your so-called enemies.

When you are distracted by material things, keep very calm, keep very still. Remember the Brethren of the Silence, whose very power of achievement lies in silence. Touch the Silence, and the power of the spirit will flow into you and disperse all your fears.

Dispassion

The Master has said that one of the essentials for a disciple is to reach a state of dispassion, a tranquil state of being. Nothing delays the progress of a soul on the path so much as lack of dispassion. It is perhaps easy to enter into this state while you are living in prepared and harmonious conditions. But it is not so easy when you return to a world of turmoil, because although you may try to retain inward peace, you are still subject to the violent vibrations of humanity in the outer world. Nevertheless, dispassion is something to which every disciple must attain, for without it he or she cannot maintain close communion with the Master. On this is built all true and devotional work. So, while you seek to meditate, let all outer things fall from you: surrender your mind, your soul and your body to the joys of the spiritual life, and in time you will be able to remain dispassionate even in the turmoil?

What do we mean? You probably know already. Dispassion means meeting every event of human life with tranquillity, knowing that all things result from one's own failure or achievement, and every event therefore comes along for good. We may not like it. We may exclaim, 'This sorrow will break my heart. How can God be a God of love when He sends such things?'. But God's love is so much greater than our human conception of love, and God sends these things into human life in order to give the soul an opportunity to strengthen itself and to meet events with tranquillity of spirit, never doubting that whatever happens is for the soul's good.

Throughout your Bible, there are stories of people who were tested almost beyond endurance but who came through. One of them was Job, who seemed to be visited with all kinds of sorrows until everything was taken from him. Even his body was a mass of festering sores; but he still held fast to the love of God, and so he passed the test. He knew that whatever happened was either because he deserved it, or to test him for his final initiation.

Will you visualize the form of the white lotus? Let us see this flower as resting upon the surface of the stilled waters, its roots reaching down into the mud beneath.

Let us see in this symbol a deep truth, as representative of the soul which has become at peace, that is stilled, untouched by the storms and passions of life ... the soul which has learned the lesson of dispassion.

We recognize the sensitivity which results from the increase of the spiritual forces within, which are assisted in their growth by the great rays of light and power from on high. But he or she who would become worthy of initiation into the temple of the holy mysteries must learn dispassion. Such a person must learn to be unaffected, undisturbed, by those things which usually cause the less understanding, or younger, soul to fly into a state of mind which must cut him or her off from those spiritual blessings of God which indeed are the birthright of all of you.

The symbol of the lotus should bring to your waiting minds this state of dispassion which you and we all seek. It is a symbol of annunciation ... of initiation. It tells those who are the silent watchers of human growth and spiritual unfoldment the moment when the soul is ready to be guided towards the gates of heaven. The lotus is a symbol of impersonal service, but also a symbol of power. The rose symbolizes human and divine love, and in the life of the Christ-person we see this complete blending. The lotus also represents this love, but a universal love, a love withdrawn from the personal. It is a complete symbol of life. We see represented in its form the six-pointed Star, within the centre of which dwells the life of God. The life of God is the central point within the six-pointed Star; while the Star as a whole stands as the complete symbol of the God-life. It is a Star of brotherhood, of power and wisdom. This is the respect in which the lotus is a symbol of power.

Standing by a lake (in the world of spirit) and watching the reflection of goodness and beauty, you can see your own reflection, and see yourself in comparison with God and God's manifestation of truth. And thus you gain the jewel of truth. It is then that the dewdrop shines within the lotus.

As we have said, this lesson of dispassion is one of the most important lessons to be learnt by the candidate treading the path towards the major initiations.

Patience

All around you, while you live in a physical body, are worlds unknown and seas uncharted. It is good when all people can be acquainted with these invisible worlds. Then they may adjust their bodies, souls and spirits to the influence of the finer ethers of the worlds of spirit from which every soul has journeyed before birth into flesh: worlds to which every soul is now journeying on the return journey to the true home of the spirit.

Only when the soul begins to understand the forces which play around it from these higher realms of life does the expansion of spiritual consciousness commence. When once this light has dawned upon a young soul, the advance upon the path is fairly rapid, according to our spiritual understanding of time.

In the earthly body, time is a master, and an unpleasant one—but only as far as *you* are concerned. Time is a great teacher, and maybe you are learning wisdom from Father Time even now. Saturn, sometimes portrayed as Father Time, is strict with his pupils, and permits no hustle, allows no hurried lessons and hasty sums and superficial essays. He insists upon a due space of time being given to every lesson; and time is one of the most irksome forms of discipline the body has to endure. Nevertheless, Saturn brings true wealth to every soul. Remember the beneficence of Saturn, and do not dwell upon the malefic influence, because you have much to thank Saturn for at present. True, the Saturnine influence makes you feel a little cold, but cold and chill is holding up and delaying the hot-headed people who would rush forward! Saturn says, 'Wait, lessons are being learned'. Those who would hurry through this unpleasantness must remember that they attempt to put aside a venerable, gracious and wise teacher. Have patience, for patience is one of the important lessons to be learnt on the path of spiritual development.

XII

PRAYER

A New Way

[*Although in parts of this teaching White Eagle is referring to communication with God and the angels in spirit, he is also speaking of our approach to the Christ within—the voice of our intuition.*]

It has been known for a spirit or an angel to visit very ordinary people at ordinary times, but usually the angels, teachers and guides come to a person when he or she is in a raised state of consciousness. The materialist may call this by other names—such as a state of hysteria or a state of trance. But then the earthly mind, mortal as it is, does not understand that beyond the physical world is a world of a finer ether, of a higher vibration. Therefore anyone who receives communication from that world must be someone able to raise his or her consciousness; or, in other words, be able to go into the 'upper room'.

Throughout all religious history, and also in the Bible, reference is made continually to the Master (or to the disciples) going up into the mountain. We are told that Jesus went up into the mountain, and when he was set his disciples came to him. This illustrates our point. There must first be this ascension to the raised state of consciousness. Then the Holy Spirit is both seen and felt. At Pentecost, the tongues of fire shone upon the disciples who were talking of their master, who were expecting some demonstration of his presence, of his continual life.[20] The truth within them was able to assert itself and tell them that the Master was near. Many other illustrations throughout the scriptures and religious history tell you that in a purified, rarefied state of life there is complete reunion and communion with those who have passed from the earth.

We have said that usually this communion (or communication) comes to those who have prepared themselves by retiring to a sanctuary or to the heights, but it does not always follow that you need seek to be alone in a church or sanctuary. You may not even realize that you are praying. Yours may be an unuttered prayer, but nonetheless a true prayer to God. The very act causes you to 'plug in' to the world of spirit; to create the necessary spiritual state which enables you to hear the voice or message of the spirit, or even to supply, from your finer bodies, an etheric substance which enables the messenger from the spirit world to clothe him or herself in form.

We do not suggest to you that you should not be sensible and well-balanced about these things. You must live on the earth in the right way. You must understand that you are here in a body for a certain purpose. You must also remember that this communication from the world of pure spirit will not be denied if you remain humble in your heart and simple in faith and trust in the eternal love. If you hear a voice which seems Godlike, true and beautiful in its wisdom, do not say, 'It is my imagination'. Remember always that no visitor from the realm above will give a message contrary to the law of Christ, nor speak words which are unkind or hurtful to another; and no such visitor will ever send you off on some wild goose chase. *By their fruits ye shall know them*.[21] The message which comes from pure spirit (or from the Christ circle) will be what you would expect to come from a state of purity, love, tenderness and wisdom. By their fruits ye shall indeed know them.' What comes from the Christ circle will bear the stamp or the hallmark of the Christ spirit. No true guide or teacher will ever give a message that is harsh, untrue or unkind. That is the test.

But here we would say that people are not always correct in their interpretation. If a message appears to be misleading or false, be patient. Wait for an explanation or an outworking of this message. Also remember that such messages sometimes apply not to material conditions but to your spiritual evolution, and the outworking or the opening of your own state of consciousness. Also remember that when you are in this higher state, or when you are functioning at the level of spiritual life, there is no time and no space and no death. The outworking of a statement at this higher level may be incomprehensible to you when you return to earthly consciousness.

We were speaking about the attunement of a person's spirit with God. Much as there are with radio waves, there are frequently interferences, so that your reception is faulty. Similar conditions prevail with the reception of pure spirit. The waves may cross. Then you get imperfect reception, while the desires of the recipient lead to a still more imperfect interpretation. You see how the message gets distorted?

The condition, then, for clear and perfect reception is one of stillness and silence, not only stillness on the outer plane but presence deep, deep, deep within the inner world, the inner place. Underneath all conflicting vibrations, beloved ones, is the Silence; and in that Silence is God. God is behind all form, all activity, all manifestation. God is *there*.

This brings us to some thoughts we would offer you on the power of prayer. We hope these few words will give you a true understanding of what prayer is, and what it can do. Remember, a little child can pray and receive a direct answer to prayer. So it does not require great intellect or intelligence to pray aright. True prayer is a projection, an earnest breathing-forth to God—to this great Silence, this enfolding and interpenetrating activity, this Life, this Spirit.

It is not wise to pray without taking thought. For prayer is a potent thing, and if the desire sent out be strong enough, it can and does reach its level. For example, you may pray for something that your desire body thinks it needs very badly. That thought can be so potent that it will bring an answer in return. Prayer can be rather like a boomerang, flying out and coming back as swiftly. The fulfilling of your desire may not always bring you happiness or blessing, but it will anyway teach you a lesson. On the other hand, if you send out an earnest prayer, a thought, a belief in faith and trust, in confidence that God your Father, the great penetrating and interpenetrating Spirit, knows your need and will answer your need, that is true prayer.

You will see that the better way is to pray not with any desire for anything, but to worship the Great Spirit of love by giving trust. 'O Father God, Thou who art all love, whatever happens is Thy will. I trust Thee, O great Mother and Son; I trust Thee. Thou wilt give according to Thy love; therefore may I, thy child, be thankful for whatever Thou sendest.' This is true prayer, 'Thy will be done in me; Thy will be done on earth as it is being done in heaven—in a state of harmony and happiness. For Thine is the kingdom, Thine is the power, Thine is the glory. May Thy glory be able to enter my heart and show me the way.'

A child, being pure in heart, may pray believing in the kindness and the love of the Father–Mother in the same way as it might believe in human parents. The divine seed in the child believes that the Father and the Mother know its need. It goes to the Father–Mother confidently. This is true prayer, and that prayer is answered. Nevertheless, we repeat, take care *how* you pray and for *what* you pray. 'Not my will, but *Thy* will be done in me, and in my life.'

This brings our last point. How should you pray for the world? Does your prayer originate from your own desire body, or do you pray for the coming of the Kingdom on earth? Do you pray for the God-life to manifest in all its glory and beauty through humanity? Now we are coming closer. Do you pray with all your daily thought and action? For that is real prayer. Right motive, right thinking, right speaking, right action—here is the greatest and the truest prayer. In this way will the disciple not only pray, but live and work for the coming of the Kingdom. So you see the importance of human conduct, of the effort to bring about the brotherhood of men and women through the brotherhood of the spirit?

The most important thing is to become so attuned that in every moment of your life you are setting in motion a chain of causation which some day is bound to have an effect upon your body, your soul, and upon life generally. Another form of prayer is thankfulness to God for everything, no matter whether it appears to be nice or the reverse. The sage accepts all things with a joyful and thankful heart. So also with you. Whatever comes, comes as a blessing from the divine love and wisdom.

Do not believe that this world around you is always

going to remain dark and ignorant. Look back no further than fifty years, and you must admit that while the growing pains may have been unpleasant, there was and is a better state of life dawning for *all* people. In the degree each one receives this spiritual truth, this ancient wisdom, and puts it into action in daily life, it must slowly penetrate national and international life. Peace on earth, brotherhood and the cessation of war and conflict is bound to come.

We assure you that the day will dawn when all countries will live together under one world government. Nations will live as brothers and sisters, helping each other on their journey: no longer hindering or warring with each other, but serving each other and beautifying the lives of millions. The day is surely dawning when this vision will come clearly to all people of goodwill. By this we mean all people who live not for self but for God and God's creation, who live to be instruments through which the life of God can manifest in all its glory.

This lies before you, children of earth. Have courage to believe. Subdue the voice of the lower self, of the earthly nature. Open your ears to the heavenly music, to the angelic choir. By this beauty your lives will be glorified and blessed.

Prayer is an aspiration of the soul to receive light, wholeness, healthiness. True prayer, true aspiration *must* be answered. If there is selfishness in the prayer, how can it be answered? Selfishness puts it out of harmony with the life of Christ. God always sends good to you to answer your prayers. You see how plainly it is stated? You cannot bear the fruit of the spirit unless you abide in Christ. There is no beauty in the spirit world for any one until he or she has learned to abide in Christ, to dwell in light, in love and brotherhood.

We would bring home the meaning of this saying of the Master: *If ye abide in me, and my words abide in you, ye shall ask what ye will and it shall be done unto you.*[22] Not in the spoken word, but in the spirit of Christ within us. Ask, seek, pray, and your prayers will be answered. But ask in the true spirit—the spirit of a child humble enough and willing to learn from its parents. *Thy* will, O God, be done—not as *I* will, but *Thy* will.

Peace

This is a simple exercise. On rising, face the rising sun, if possible, before an open window. Stand erect so that you are correctly polarised, with the spine straight; and with the solar plexus controlled. Before you take your breath, centre your concentration—it will come in a flash—upon the central Light, the golden Light if you like. You can realize this Light in your head centre. And as you realize this universal Light, this Father–Mother God, you will instantly feel in your heart a sense of love, and dependence upon the Father–Mother. Try to realize your relationship with the Great Spirit. Now take your breath. On the first day, take three deep breaths; then six; then nine, and so on; and as you breathe, breathe not only air, but life atoms into your being. Raise your arms as you breathe in, if you find it helpful, and then, as you breathe out, let your arms fall slowly.

As you inhale each breath, aspire to God. Feel that God is entering into you; as you exhale bless all life. This inbreathing will cause spiritual light, the spiritual Sun behind the physical sun, to enter into you and register on the membranes at the head centre, on the brow; and from that centre you can mentally direct the light to the heart centre, to bring spiritual water and sunlight to the seed-atom which rests in the human heart.

This rhythmic breathing does something more than affect your body. Seen clairvoyantly, the person breathing in, in full consciousness, the divine life, is radiating a great light. He or she is strengthening the soul and causing it to expand and send out feelers of light, shafts of light. You breathe in and absorb this stream of life and light from the Father–Mother God, and then you let it fall from you in blessing upon others. So you absorb God's life, and you bless all life. You receive and you give; and so you come into harmony with the rhythmic lifestream. It will feed your nerves, and give you a sense of peace and control.

Seek the will of God, and not self-will. Let all nations seek the divine will for the whole earth. No country need be anxious if it puts into operation the law of

God in all its dealings. We know that many problems will arise, but we still maintain that the spiritual law is the way of peace. Humanity, however, has yet to give this spiritual law an opportunity; and instead, people have many excuses and reasons ready why spiritual law should not be applied. This is nevertheless the only answer, and so we say: in your own life *seek first the kingdom of God*.[23] Go into the silence; seek there, and then when you have found it, let it manifest in your own lives.

On this path, the graph goes up and down. Keep on persevering with your everyday life and your set lessons, thereby bringing this light within into conscious operation, so that the very cells of your body become finer. This is what is happening in the world. Spirit—God—is continually moulding, purifying, raising the world's vibrations.

What takes place in the individual in the form of karma, opportunity and spiritual evolution, is taking place throughout the life of nations, in planets, in whole solar systems, all in obedience to a law of unfoldment and growth. We could almost describe it as a breathing-in and breathing-out, a rhythmic breathing. Normally the physical process of breathing is so harmonious and gentle that you do not feel yourself breathe. This is what God is doing. All the time, the God-life is moving into humanity and then withdrawing, coming into incarnation, passing out of incarnation. Ages come and then they sink away. They come up again. Life is one continual rhythm, and the whole of life is striving towards perfection and still more perfection. Can perfection ever end? No, there is a continual beautification. If you can think of a panoramic scene which is continually, gradually unfolding and unfolding so that you never come to its end, you might get the idea.

NOTES

[1] White Eagle speaks of his own mission as a teacher 'on the ray of St John' in the book, THE LIGHT BRINGER (W.E.P.T., 2001).

[2] The temples built for worship in the White Eagle Lodge are intended as an imitation of the great universal temple that White Eagle here foresees. The biblical quotation that follows is from Acts 2 : 17.

[3] White Eagle elsewhere (e.g. WALKING WITH THE ANGELS (W.E.P.T., 1998)) lists the rays as follows. The first is the ray of power or will, the second that of love or philanthropy; the third that of wisdom or philosophy. Then there is the balancing fourth ray of harmony, followed by another wisdom ray (that of science); another of love (the sixth ray, the ray of the mystic) and another of power (the seventh, that of ceremonial and beauty). When he speaks of the love–wisdom ray, he evidently intends a blending of two or more of these rays.

[4] Throughout his teaching White Eagle uses the term 'the Christ' to indicate the universal Being who manifested through Jesus Christ, rather than Jesus himself.

[5] Matthew 22 : 37–39

[6] This passage also occurs in THE LIGHT BRINGER, p. 115.

[7] Mark 4 : 37–39.

[8] Luke 4 : 11, quoting Psalm 91 :12.

[9] White Eagle seems to mean the following: the physical body, the elemental (which is also the vital body), the astral (which is also